OUR DAILY BREAD

To Claire

Enjoy my book,

with Every Blessing.

Fr Alec
x

FATHER ALEX FROST

WITH CATHRYN KEMP

OUR DAILY BREAD

FROM ARGOS TO THE ALTAR.
A PRIEST'S STORY

Harper
North

HarperNorth
Windmill Green
Mount Street
Manchester M2 3NX

A division of
HarperCollins*Publishers*
1 London Bridge Street
London SE1 9GF

www.harpercollins.co.uk

HarperCollinsPublishers
1st Floor, Watermarque Building, Ringsend Road
Dublin 4, Ireland

First published by HarperNorth in 2022

1 3 5 7 9 10 8 6 4 2

A catalogue record for this book is
available from the British Library

ISBN: 978-0-00-855652-5

Printed and bound in the UK using 100%
renewable electricity at CPI Group (UK) Ltd

MIX
Paper | Supporting
responsible forestry
FSC™ C007454
FSC
www.fsc.org

This book is produced from independently certified FSC™ paper
to ensure responsible forest management.

For more information visit: www.harpercollins.co.uk/green

To Mark, the Devlin Family, Jenny Swears-a-Lot
and my hometown of Burnley.

Without these people this book
would not have possible

#UTC

'Give us this day our daily bread'

Matthew 6:11

CONTENTS

CONTENTS

FOREWORD

'We don't do God' is perhaps the most oft-repeated soundbite of my time in politics. It is often interpreted as an anti-faith statement. It is not and was never intended as such. It was my way of saying I did not believe that the public like to see politicians relate their faith to their politics. Indeed, I am a pro-faith atheist. I don't do God myself, though my believing sister Liz constantly assures me 'God does you.'

I am also extremely pro people of God who do good. And Fr Alex is very much in that category. That became all too clear in the powerful BBC News documentary *The Cost of Covid: A Year on the Front Line*. The documentary focused both on his work, and on that of Pastor Mick Fleming from Church on the Street Ministries, showing the many families affected by extreme poverty in Burnley, Lancashire.

Like millions of people, I was deeply moved by the film, and horrified to witness the levels of deprivation that have hit parts of the North, and indeed many parts of the UK. Sadly, it didn't come as any great surprise, as I have been concerned, and publicly vocal, about the austerity measures that have crippled much of Britain before, during and since the global pandemic. It was hard not to be affected by the stories and people featured in this news item, and I was delighted to see the piece recognised at the recent RTS awards.

Fr Alex and I share a passion for football. We are both dedicated supporters of Burnley Football Club and have followed the club for decades. We have seen times of great success, including a number of years in the Premier League, a brief foray into European football, and the spectacular development of the infrastructure of our ground 'Turf Moor' with training facilities on the edge of town near to the beautiful Gawthorpe Hall. We also both know what it is to suffer as fans of the Clarets and have both lived through the club's numerous failures and near-misses, though with some exceptions, including the nail-biting encounter that saw Burnley narrowly beat Orient FC in May 1987 to retain our place in the football league.

I had also spotted Alex on social media where he hosts his aptly named podcast, 'The God Cast', and was delighted to accept an invitation, not least so I could adapt that soundbite to 'I don't do God, but I do The God Cast'. Despite being interviewed thousands of times by journalists in the media, which can make me a bit bored and formulaic, I found our discussion a refreshing, and at times fearless, one. It isn't often I'm asked to talk about God or faith and asked to do so in such a spirit of compassion and empathy. This way of speaking in the public eye is perhaps a challenge to all politicians to seek the common ground, to argue better, as Fr Alex goes on to discuss in this timely and important book. I was struck by Alex's remarks, so much so that I mentioned him in an article I wrote for the *Independent* in December 2020.

Fr Alex's call for a kinder, compassionate approach to politics, and life, shouldn't be under-estimated. This book has numerous accounts of kindness overcoming greed, action overcoming austerity, and dare I say it, light overcoming the darkness. Fr Alex's skill is that he does his work with humour, empathy and a down-to-earth, approachable spirituality. While I may not feel called to be a weekly disciple at the foot of the cross, I deeply respect and admire those who are, and understand that for many people spiritual wellbeing is as essential to wellbeing as anything else.

Fr Alex's reminder that 'poverty' extends far beyond financial scarcity is an important matter to be considered if the current government's 'Levelling Up' agenda is ever to be truly lived out as an aspiration that is achievable and not merely end up as yet another slogan devoid of substance. Fr Alex makes the point that before 'tarted up' town centres and renovated clock faces, priority should be given to those who need it most, and frankly I couldn't agree more.

Our Daily Bread is a unique and rare insight into the work of an urban parish priest. Without the Church's engagement with such matters of social injustice and voluntary support, many places would be in a much graver situation than they already are. Fr Alex gives a true picture of what it is like when people on the fringes of society get left behind or forgotten about. The stories at times are deeply moving and harrowing, and one cannot fail to reflect on the impact that the pandemic and cost-of-living crisis are having on some of Britain's most deprived communities. And yet, Fr Alex also manages to draw out something of these communities that brings hope and inspiration. Amid the unfairness and injustice, there is also humour, love and togetherness, restoring hope in and towards humankind and the solutions that involve spiritual serenity.

This book is an essential read for anyone who believes poverty doesn't exist. It is an essential read for anyone who believes the societal landscape is already level, and it's an absolute must-read for anyone who believes that the Church doesn't have an essential role to play in effecting change and calling out injustice.

Fr Alex and I probably won't live long enough to see Burnley lift the Premier League Trophy and win a place in the Champions League, but we certainly share the same aspiration that people living in poverty shouldn't need to wait a lifetime for change to happen. I applaud Fr Alex for speaking out as frankly as he does; I applaud him for sticking his head above the parapet and being brave enough to hold politicians and the Church to account when they fail the people of our great country.

It would be my hope that politicians, journalists and broadcasters read this book and consider what they could do differently to change the road map that affects so many of our estates and urban settings. What actions can they take that might change the destination of travel for places where addiction, crime, abuse have become almost normalised over many years under the stewardship of politicians of all persuasion? Who will make a difference? How will they make a difference? And, most importantly, when will they make a difference?

These are stark and important questions that urgently need answers. Fr Alex is a hardworking Church of England priest. He says himself that he doesn't have all the answers, but he deserves our thanks for asking the questions.

Alastair Campbell, May 2022

PROLOGUE

BLESSED

'Blessed are you who are poor,
as yours is the kingdom of God.
Blessed are you who are hungry now,
as you will be filled.
Blessed are you who eat now,
for you will laugh.'

Luke 6: 20–21

In the darkest days of the pandemic, people from the estates that spread out from around St Matthew's the Apostle Church in Burnley queued in the bitter cold for makeshift food parcels handed out in a car park by me and another clergyman, Pastor Mick Fleming. People who'd lost their jobs, who were ill and cold in wheelchairs, who were isolated and alone, and who could not afford to feed their kids or warm their homes, waited, sometimes impatiently, for a bag of cheap pasta and a few tins of baked beans. In Luke's Gospel it says 'Blessed are the poor.' Well I can tell you, they don't feel very fucking blessed, and I didn't see anyone laughing that night as we handed out the food donated by our community. In fact, if you've ever seen news reports on the telly of the Red Cross handing out food from the back of a lorry in Syria or Rwanda, then you've got an idea of the need and the chaos we have seen on the streets of modern Britain.

As a priest, I get to walk in the shoes of some of society's poorest, most deprived and suffering people in the beloved northern town I call home. I get to walk the streets of the estates I've come to love, and the people I've come to admire in all their resilient, vulnerable, brazen glory. Amid these once-cobbled roads that are lined with Coronation Street-style terraced houses and run-down council homes. I get to live the gospel of Jesus Christ, which tells us, simply, to help the needy and love thy neighbour. This is a place where people shop in their pyjamas, where Christmas lights go up in October to bring some kind of cheer, where disagreements are often played out publicly in front yards with fights or loud arguments, where the police force and Social Services are frequent visitors. It is a place where people learn early on about survival, where school is a passing interlude between the business of eking out a living, where you learn which families are not to be messed with, and where grassing people up is the worst crime. It might be more George from Asda than Georgio Armani, but it is a place of real beauty. There is community here. All the families know each other and people look out for each other. It is a place where kids play on the streets until it gets dark, and where fireworks go off all year round to honour loved ones who have died. If you weren't born into poverty, or didn't grow up on one of Britain's urban estates, you might associate a place like this with all the negative stereotypes. You might imagine that all the mums are single parents, that every other house is a shit hole and everyone is living on state benefits. While this is true in many cases, it isn't true of everyone, as the people you'll read about in these pages demonstrate. They have challenges, which you'll also read about – drug problems, having to feed their kids on one wage, struggles paying the bills, facing all sorts of anti-social behaviour – but they are people with big hearts and souls who are, in turn, humorous, frustrating, loving and, at times, completely impossible to figure out. Being a priest has given me special access to this community, where an outsider is usually an outsider for a long time before being trusted. I honour that trust deeply, and I know it is a privilege, which I do not take lightly.

I wasn't born into a religious family but instead came to the Church at the ripe old age of 40, bemused and wondering what the bloody hell had happened to make me want to wear a dog collar. Well, God happened. Jesus' word happened, and now I am his disciple. I practise what I preach by running foodbanks for the neediest, by attempting to follow the gospel and help those who most need it. My faith wasn't indoctrinated into me. My formation as a Christian crept up on me. It made gentle introductions, it left subtle deposits, just as my puppy does sometimes. Slowly but surely, I arrived at a place of acceptance, tranquillity and spirituality. That spiritual place ultimately led me to a physical place, which was St Matthew's Church. It is a place of real joy, of pain and of suffering, and God has been there in all of it, from beginning to end.

Burnley has its fair share of problems. It sits within the most deprived 10 per cent of lower-tier local authorities in England, according to a report published in 2019 by the

Ministry of Housing, Communities and Local Government (MHCLG). It sits within the 20 per cent of the most health-deprived and high-disability areas in the Lancashire-12 area. Trinity and Bank Hall wards in Burnley are the most deprived in the whole of the county. If you think that 55 per cent of our children qualify for free school meals (rapacious austerity measures saw to that) then you can see we are a community on the edge, permanently on the brink of disaster. Then, the pandemic happened and the fall-out has been catastrophic.

In light of the scenes of utter misery and deprivation as people were handed out food bags from our pop-up foodbank in a Burnley car park, what do the words of Luke, above, mean? No one could look at the people in my parish, pushing each other at times to try and get to the front of the queue so they'd have something to eat that night, and say 'blessed are the poor', could they? It's a challenging one to unpack. To my mind, poverty, or poorness, isn't just about financial deprivation; it is spiritual poverty, emotional poverty, poverty of aspiration, poverty of evolution in people's lives, poverty of wellbeing. It is about people being forced to live in appalling housing conditions, owing money to loan sharks or having spiralling debt. It is about people who are suffering from mental or physical health issues, or having a poor education, few job prospects and at the mercy of overwhelmed support services. It is very easy to be a disciple, to follow Jesus' message, when the sun is shining and things are going well, but what about when they aren't? What about when we are faced with suffering, when we are faced with trauma or grief or being unable to feed our kids? What then?

I refuse to normalise the depths of deprivation I come into contact with each day. It's beyond poverty – it's destitution. I see mums who have to decide between replacing a broken kettle and feeding their children. I hear terrible stories of people left in crisis for months on NHS mental health waiting lists. I see first-hand the impact of benefit delays or cuts.

In the Bible, the Beatitudes (blessings) that proclaim the way of Jesus go much further than simple blessing. They ask for total transformation; a profound change in all our attitudes, and nowhere is this more important than on the front line of modern urban poverty in Britain. I believe the passage from Luke is referring to those who are suffering when he uses the word 'poor'. I believe he is saying, blessed are the suffering. What I think Jesus was referring to was that we have a capacity to learn from our experience of suffering and to evolve through it. Sometimes, I feel as a society we have lost the skill of being able to pause, to observe, to witness, to appreciate the imperfections of life. Those suffering are blessed because they can bring empathy, compassion and kindness to others. If you've been through a shitty situation, it enables you to be gentle and compassionate to those who are in trouble. This message in Luke's Gospel only really came home to me, I only really understood it, when my dad was diagnosed with vascular dementia. Over the weeks and months, I watched him change, I watched him deteriorate and I was so angry about his illness. Dad absconded from hospital, took a taxi in his pyjamas back to Worsthorne, the village he lived in with my mum, but he couldn't remember the address. A villager recognised him and he was okay but had to be sectioned for tests to be carried out. I saw the progression of the condition when I visited him in the secure ward. He tried to manipulate the doctors by asking me to tell them he could leave. I'd promise him I would and so he'd go to the bathroom to get changed, thinking he was going home, and I'd have to leave, get to my car where I would break down in tears. I was allowed to take him out one day, so I took him to Morrison's for some soup and a chat. He shat himself, which made his trousers fall down. I felt utterly helpless. Nobody came to help. I hoisted up his pants and cleaned him up as best I could in the toilets, but it was undignified, and it wasn't long before he went into full-time care after that incident. I hated that. I hated him being in care. He was incontinent and he'd always be blocking the toilet because he'd try to flush his underpants away.

Yet I still saw beauty in his journey. My dad was a brilliant pianist, and one day when I watched him play on the piano in the care home, his beautiful hands remembering the notes, I saw his illness float away and for those ten minutes I got my dad back. At that time, a decade ago now, I was in the midst of my training to be a priest. By then, I knew God was in this process. A few weeks later my family and I were away in Wales on holiday when my brother rang me and said that Dad was slipping away. We raced back, and I had the chance to sit with him, to witness his suffering. His breathing was going up and down, and then it became really shallow and I knew it was the end. I felt I was being given something, something vital, something important by God. Dad was in his darkest hour and I was being given the chance to sit and reflect on all the things he meant to me. My dad had taught me so much: his kindness, his compassion, everything he was to me. So, when he died, I didn't feel angry and I wasn't hysterical. There was no massive wave of grief; I simply felt joy, and I felt thankful that his suffering had come to an end. I kissed his forehead and told him I loved him. I sat in the conservatory in the chair he used to sit on and I prayed, I laughed to myself, I remembered. I gave thanks to God for everything he'd given me. In my darkest hour, I felt incredibly blessed, which is why I feel able to suggest that Jesus meant something similar by 'blessed are the poor'. If we rephrase it, 'blessed are the suffering', then I understand that I've been blessed by my suffering, and this knowledge has given so much to my ministry as a priest. When I listen and speak to the poorest in my community, I know that serving them is a blessing. I can support people with empathy because I have suffered, and this is the teaching Jesus gives us. Do Jesus' words from Luke's Gospel translate into our contemporary world? I think they do. I witness beauty as well as pain, joy as well as suffering, and this is my blessing, this is my work and the work our state church has to step up and do. Daily, I experience hope and inspiration from the very people whom society has forgotten. Daily, I learn more from those who call me to assist or serve them. In my ministry, I see people on a weekly basis who are considered financially poor yet in spirit are far from it. These are the people who feed my soul, who bless me with the honour of serving them. I didn't see God leading me down this pathway, to do what I do and be with the people I am with. If my dad hadn't been through the horror of dementia, I'm not sure I would be the person I am today, nor have the ministry I have today. Jesus tells us it starts with the broken, the damaged, the poor. It is a deeply theological idea of meaning and worth, and yet he is just telling us that we start by looking after the poor, and we go from there. They are the priority, and those who suffer perhaps have the most to offer us as a society.

BBC News came and filmed us at St Matthew's Church at the peak of the pandemic, during lockdown, as we were handing out hundreds of food parcels to people who otherwise might not be able to afford to eat. The documentary they made, *The Cost of Covid: A Year on the Front Line*, went on to win the News Coverage – Home category of the RTS Television Journalism Awards 2022, and it has been viewed more than 14 million times since it was aired in 2021. Some of the people featured are those whose stories I share in this book. The stories are all true. They're all real people dealing with things that most of us in our nice homes with nice families and good jobs, hopefully, won't ever have to deal with. I am honoured that the people in these pages have given me their blessing to tell their truths, their stories, their journeys. A lot of what I'm able to share with you is private, it's deeply intimate and, sometimes, extremely harrowing. Yet, they want me to tell their tales. What courage this shows from people who know they're at the bottom of the heap. What trust to be able to open up about their lives and the often-difficult paths they are walking. I know many of them hope that in telling their stories they might, finally, be heard. And, actually, who else is listening to these people? I would argue that no one is. I understand why. If those souls who have the privilege of running our country ever stepped foot inside my foodbank, they would be greeted by uncomfortable truths. They would see what living life on the edge, on the fringes of society, does to people. I have written to our own current member of Parliament, Conservative MP Antony Higginbotham, several times, asking why the government has withdrawn some of the measures to help the homeless, and inviting him to the foodbank at St Matthew's Church where I am proud to be vicar. I have told him that each person in desperate need has a story to tell, and yes, they are depressed, rejected and forgotten but they are also intelligent and vibrant.

We have yet to receive a visit.

Is this good enough? I would argue, passionately, that it isn't. It isn't good enough if those elected to represent us appear to represent only a percentage of their constituents, if they continue to ignore those at the bottom, for how will the latter ever find their way up to a better life, to a decent job, to self-respect, to money in their wallets, to thriving? I'd like our local MP to come to our foodbank. I'd like him to come and see the most deprived area of the town and spend some time with the people here. I don't expect him – or anyone – to wave a magic wand, but I do expect something more than rhetoric. Come and see the nitty-gritty; the entertaining, funny, fierce and sometimes harrowing world these people inhabit. I would love to invite the prime minister or the leader of the opposition to come and walk these streets with me. To speak from the head is not the same as speaking from the heart. If they see it with their eyes, if they can feel it in their hearts, then they might just get it. And if they get it, they can make a difference. Until that happens, I fear the estates will forever be a place where communities suffer hardship, where children don't progress, where people remain trapped in cycles of poverty, addiction and apathy.

It is the privilege of my life to help people navigate the brutal, soul-sapping, gut-punching post-austerity, post-pandemic world. This isn't just a 'Burnley problem', nor a 'northern problem'; grass-roots poverty is widespread throughout the UK, and is only going to get worse as we sink deeper into a cost-of-living crisis that is unprecedented in our lifetimes. Just as importantly, spiritual poverty in the form of lethargy, hopelessness, anxiety and depression is rife among people from all walks of life. Who are we any more? Didn't we all start to ask that question during the pandemic? What kind of a country are we? Do we celebrate difference and open our hearts to all the unique gifts people bring, or are we intolerant, exclusive, small-hearted towards those who don't immediately appear to have much to offer? To my mind, the real pandemic is that no one actually cares about those floundering at the edges.

This is a book about modern poverty, the type that shouldn't still exist if we actually took on board the teachings Jesus gave us. It's simple really – we can help the needy or we can leave them to drown in an uncaring world where profits mean more than people, where the poor pay for the mistakes of the rich with benefits cuts, rent hikes and zero hours contracts. We have to support them to get better, little by little. To me, there's no choice.

Predictions are that millions more people will be driven by the escalating cost-of-living crisis into 'absolute poverty' as energy, food and oil prices rise. The forecast is even bleaker for those already struggling to make ends meet in the most deprived households. Absolute poverty has been defined by the UN World Summit for Economic Development as a 'condition characterised by severe deprivation of basic human needs, including food, safe drinking water, sanitation facilities, health, shelter, education and information. It depends not only on income but on access to services.' The Joseph Rowntree Foundation, cited in an article by the *Independent* newspaper, defines it this way: 'Poverty means not being able to heat your home, pay your rent or buy the essentials for your children. It means waking up every day facing insecurity, uncertainty and impossible decisions about money. It means facing marginalisation – and even discrimination – because of your financial circumstances.' My response to that is: 'Welcome to Burnley, mate!'

1.

MARK

'If anyone causes one of these little ones –
those who believe in me – to stumble, it would be
better for them to have a large millstone hung
around their neck and to be drowned in the
depths of the sea.'

Matthew 18:6

Twitching and paranoid, the man shuffled in to St Matthew's one dreary autumn morning, scrabbling in his pocket for something, money perhaps, or a tissue to wipe his bloodied face. He didn't have to say that he was struggling; his black eye, a broken nose and puffy skin, his bedraggled hair and unshaven chin, dirt-encrusted nails and the stench of alcohol told me everything I needed to know. He sat down heavily, clearly in a bad way: his hands were trembling, his clothes were unkempt, dirty and ragged, and it looked to me like he was dealing with some heavy-duty demons. I kept my distance because not everyone who comes in to church wants to speak to a vicar, and so I generally hold back, or if someone seems like they want to chat, I'll go and say: 'Alright, how are ye?'

After a while, Mark managed to get himself out of his chair then shuffle outside. His gait was unsteady and his head and shoulders were drooping, and instinctively I followed him out. Sure enough, he was sitting on the wall underneath our cherry blossom tree so I went over and said hello and plonked myself down next to him. For a moment, neither of us spoke, and again, Mark's hand was shaking as he rubbed his short, bedraggled hair, and I guessed he was thinking about his next drink. The view outside of the church is typical Burnley: industrious, noisy, busy with passers-by. We're surrounded by the streets and alleys of the town centre, sprawling out from around us. Rows and rows of 'two-up, two-down' terraces line the streets that have drifting bits of rubbish, the odd bit of graffiti, dog shit and a fair few knackered old cars dumped or parked badly. There are generally people, mostly men it seems, milling about, cans in hand, just like Mark. He was now clutching a can of strong lager, which I hadn't noticed before. Perhaps that's what he'd been searching for in the pockets of his ripped coat.

'You alright?' I said, not looking at him. He clearly wasn't but I wasn't going to say that. If I remember rightly, I was watching a couple of lads kick a ball in the street. We're passionate about footie up here, and Burnley Football Club is more like a religion than a sport, so it wasn't an unusual sight. I wanted to listen to whatever this guy had to say because I could see there was plenty that wasn't going well in his life. He took a swig of the beer and shrugged.

'Not really, Vicar,' was all he said. 'I'm not rait happy, no.'

'Why's that then? What's to do?' I replied, glancing over at him. He was drinking Special Brew and his whole body seemed to shake a little.

'Cos I'm havin' to live rough, like. I'm not safe where I am, they're always pickin' on me and I get hurt.' He gazed back over the overflowing rubbish bins lining the street.

For a moment, I didn't know what to say. In a transient community such as ours, people tend to come and go, sofa surfing on mates' floors or couches as they have no permanent accommodation. I didn't usually get to hear what it was like, and perhaps it was that fact that made me persevere with this guy with the battered face, though it was more probably the likelihood that this would be the only time I'd ever get to speak to him.

'I can see that,' I said. 'So where are ye sleepin'?'

Mark shrugged again.

'Oh here and there, sometimes with me mates and sometimes I go back, but I feel like chucking it all in at times, I won't lie to ye.'

That took my breath away. I tried to think what to reply, but I am someone who knows my limitations. I'm not a trained social worker. I'm not a counsellor nor a drugs and alcohol worker. I'm a priest and yet I have to find words to respond at times like this.

'Does that help?' I asked as Mark gulped down the entire can of beer. This time, Mark shook his head and a small chuckle escaped from his lips.

'Not really, Vicar. I don't feel it no more. The days of gettin' drunk are long gone; it just keeps me steady now.'

I nodded. I'd heard of that before: that with chronic alcoholism it gets to the point where the alcohol doesn't affect people in the same way. I also knew that this might be a symptom of something nasty, like liver disease, but again, I wasn't qualified to say that. I'm just a priest, I'm not a doctor and I'm wasn't there to fix this man, yet there was something about him I liked, despite his problems and his situation.

'What's your name? I'm Father Alex.'

'My name's Mark,' he said, and actually smiled.

'It's good to meet ye, Mark. Welcome to St Matthew's.'

Suddenly, there was a loud roar of an engine from across the road and we both turned to see what was going on. It was yet another off-road motorbike with its rider probably making their way to the estate's footie pitches to carve up council wasteland. Mark turned to me and, though I hadn't known him until a few moments ago, he suddenly clutched my arm.

'Can ye take me inside to the High Altar?' he begged. 'Can ye take me to sanctuary and pray for me because I'm fuckin' drowning. I'm drowning and I feel like I'm goin' to die.'

My heart went out to him. If there was a way I could have fixed this man's life here and now, I would've done it. At least, I could offer him something, and that something was prayer.

'Of course, I can, Mark. Come with me.'

I walked the man, this trembling, suffering soul, this chronic alcoholic who said he was drowning, who was terri-fied that his life might be almost over, into St Matthew's Church. It never fails to astonish me with its architectural beauty and its rich history of worship. Though the original church, which was built in 1876 in St Matthew Street, was burnt down in 1927, it was rebuilt as the existing building and we still have many of the old Anglo-Catholic traditions, such as singing, lots of candles, occasional incense and wearing traditional vestments. People often misunderstand the differences between Catholic and Protestant. In a nutshell, Roman Catholics look to the Pope for guidance as they believe the Pope is God's senior representative on earth. Some Protestants are also quite closely aligned to the Roman Catholic Church and its traditions, and after a number of years I find myself somewhere in the middle. It all gets very complicated if you are not 'churchy', but while there are things that divide the two churches, there are many that unite us. I feel comfortable in the Church of England, because it is a broader church. I enjoy the more traditional aspects of worship, like regular Holy Communion, wearing all the colourful vestments, and occasionally sanctifying the church atmosphere with a good dousing of incense. All these things are commonly associated with a more Catholic approach to worship, but the CofE is a big umbrella under which many styles and traditions of worship can flourish. St Matthew's was reopened by the Bishop of Blackburn and sits in the diocese of Blackburn. The High Altar is situated at the far end of the church in the chancel. It sits under three tall, thin windows – beneath which I often conduct morning or evening prayer – that stream light in on sunny days. We passed the series of arches that sit either side of the aisle, and rows of wooden chairs (we don't have pews), and our footsteps rang on the polished floor. Even as we walked, Mark kept repeating: 'I'm drowning, I'm drowning ...'

Kneeling in front of the golden cross, we prayed together and there was a sense of peace even though it would most likely be short-lived. I always feel a sense of wonder as I approach the High Altar, as if somehow, just by being there, things make more sense.

'God, please look over my friend Mark here in his difficulties. Please let him know he is not alone in facing his problems and watch over him, please God.'

My prayer wasn't complicated, it was a simple request for Mark to have spiritual comfort and to feel he was looked after in some way, when it was clear to me that such care was lacking in the rest of his life. I knew that all I could offer was some kind of reassurance that he wasn't lost or wasn't a hopeless case, though everything about him looked to the contrary. I wasn't going to give him platitudes though. I wasn't going to say everything was all right, because it clearly wasn't. I was there to listen as best I could. Just then, Mark began to weep. He broke down completely, and started to share some details about his past experiences. This is always a huge honour for me, to be trusted enough to hear about someone's life, their troubles, their grief and pain, as much as I rejoice when I hear people's joy and happiness.

'I got married here, Father Alex. Oh, many years ago now, but it were a beautiful ceremony. It didn't work between us, the booze always got in the way, but we tried, Father, we did try.'

Something about this made me feel utterly heartbroken for this man, who had tried to live a normal life and tried to have a marriage and a wife. He had tried to build a life for himself, yet here he was, dishevelled and beaten, questioning whether he even wanted to live.

When we'd finished praying, Mark leaned over and touched me gently on my chest.

'You're my angel,' he said, his eyes filling with tears. I shook my head.

'I'm not your angel, Mark, I'm just here to try and help,' I replied. It was Mark's turn to shake his head.

'No, you're my angel,' he repeated. 'You're all angels here.'

When we'd finished, he picked up his bag, his single posses-sion, and walked off back down the aisle that he'd walked up all those years earlier. I watched him go, amazed in some ways that he was alive at all. He looked battered. His face really did tell a thousand stories as it were bruised from the continuous assaults he must have been suffering living rough. Half his moustache was missing, possibly caused by the stress and anxiety, and he walked with a wobble. He looked abso-lutely exhausted by life, and when I later reflected upon that encounter, I thought there was something of the lost sheep about Mark. He seemed to me to be someone who had been short of love and encouragement for a very long time, which made him appear like a child in an adult's body. Over the years, I've met hundreds, perhaps thousands, of people through my ministry, but Mark seemed to get under my skin even from that brief meeting, and in the days afterwards I couldn't stop thinking about him.

After he left, I just went back to the altar and wept. I was pretty sure he was only a year or two older than me, yet our lives couldn't have been more different. Our directions of travel had been very different to one another's and it made me appreciate my life even more and feel extremely sad that his had gone so astray. Even so, I expected never to see him again; so many people passed through the church like ships in the night, and for many, learning their name was as much as I ever knew about them.

But Mark came back. He turned up again the following Saturday for a food bag, and we sat down again together and had another chat. It's a real privilege when this happens, and it is a privilege reserved for the clergy as we have no axe to grind, no forms to fill out, no testing of any kind to bring to the encounter. This time, we sat together inside the church. There were quite a few people there that day, but I really wanted to connect with him and see how he was doing.

'How are ye? Are ye alright?' I said.

'Not too bad, Father Alex,' was his reply, though he looked pretty much the same. Same ragged clothes, same battered face and broken nose. This time he showed me one of his tattoos. The man was covered in them, but he had a small one – '9%' – tattooed behind his right ear.

'So, that's me nine per cent, me Strong Brew, and I tattooed it because it keeps me goin'.'

'It keeps ye goin', Mark?' I queried. It wasn't a great tattoo. It looked a bit smudged and had probably been done fairly cheaply, I'd imagine. One of my heroes, Dave Gahan from Depeche Mode, said that his tattoos were like 'war paint' and each one marked 'a time and place' in his life. I wasn't so sure that was the reason for Mark's.

'Yeah, and all me mates have had it done too,' Mark continued, and I guessed, in that small gesture, that tribal connection, how desperately he must want to fit in, no matter where or with whom. I also thought it strange that he celebrated the millstone of drink that continues to this day to hang round his neck, though I could see that it was as much about fitting in to the crowd he hung around with as anything else.

Mark fidgeted on the seat as he gazed around, but I wanted to learn more about him, and by trying to understand him better I reasoned I could try and help him better.

'So, do ye have any family, Mark?' I asked.

Mark shrugged and his expression became almost instantly sad.

'I've got a daughter who lives in America. She's doin' well, she's doin' good. My son, well, he's in prison.'

'What about your parents? Are they local? Are they still alive?'

'We haven't spoken for a long time. We don't see each other. They live on the coast but we don't talk ...'

I could see by Mark's expression, and the drop in his voice, that this was painful to talk about and sometimes I have to make the decision to gently back off as I don't want my conversations with people to bring back memories they don't wish to revisit. It was clear that Mark appeared to have no one and nothing, and this made me feel very sad indeed. In fact, the absence of loved ones showed me the gap that existed, the gap that he no doubt filled with alcohol – a comfort that was just not working for him if it ever had. Over the following months, he talked many times about his experiences, and I have learnt much about the suffering caused by untreated alcoholism. He tells me that he wakes up each day around 5am or 6am, profusely sweating, retching and shaking. Often, he has soiled his bed. Frequently, he experiences fitting and convulsing, and if he gets a few hours' sleep a night then he's done well. This is no life for anyone, to my mind, and the more I learnt about this man's troubles, the more I wanted to help him find a way out of them.

Mark became a regular, appearing every Saturday morning, and he was always keen to make contact. I wasn't sure how to proceed though. He was often the last person to leave when we shut. He'd frequently ask me to slip him a few quid so he could buy a can of his 'nine per cent', and it's really difficult with an alcoholic to know what to do in such a situation. I knew enough to understand that if he carried on that way he'd die; at the same time, his body was so dependent upon that stuff that if he didn't get his hands on it, he'd become very ill and possibly die as well. Each time he asks, I act with discretion and make a calculated decision whether to hand over that three quid or not. Sometimes I've given in and handed it to him, but mostly I tell him 'No' and not to ask me again, which of course he always does.

Mark is an articulate and intelligent man underneath the years of neglect and addiction, which I think is what haunts me the most. I am clear in my role towards him. I am a vicar and I have the gospel of Jesus to guide me, which tells me to help the needy and to love my neighbour, which is what I have to do, even those who at first appear unlovable, like Mark. I have always known that I couldn't offer him much more than a listening ear, but it has never stopped me wanting more for him, for him to find recovery. Perhaps my own experience of having Obsessive Compulsive Disorder, OCD, as a child means I can relate in some small way to Mark's predicament. As a youngster, when I was at school, I became addicted to switching off electrical sockets. I know it sounds trivial compared to something as serious as a full-blown addiction like Mark's, but I do know that part of my life was damaging to me. I couldn't leave a room without obsessively checking the light switches. It got to a point where I had difficulty leaving the house as I had to check every switch. I knew I had to do something as it was getting out of hand, and so I made myself stop. I weaned myself off this behaviour by reducing the number of times I allowed myself to check the switches each day. It was really hard but, somehow, I did it as I knew the condition had the potential to rule my life. I was lucky to be able to do that. In the case of long-term alcoholism, I can see that breaking the cycle can be almost impossible.

Mark said something that really resonated with me, though. He said that every time he drinks a can, he swears to himself that he'll never do it again, and that was exactly what I used to tell myself. Being addicted to turning off electrical sockets was unlikely to kill me but it affected my life, whereas Mark is still doing something on a daily basis that affects his life and has the possibility of killing him as well.

In Jesus' time they used to carry out executions, and one of the methods used was literally drowning someone with a millstone around their neck. It was a brutal and frightening way to exact a punishment for wrongdoing, but those were brutal days. Alcohol is that millstone for my friend Mark. It is the weight around his neck that is threatening to drown him, yet I feel there is hope for Mark. He talks with honesty about his troubles, and doesn't ever shy away from his problems, and that, to me, is the seed for something. Jesus in the words above meant that to be drowned with a millstone around your neck would be a fate preferable to going to hell. As anyone in Alcoholics Anonymous knows, Mark is already in the latter, and the only way now is up, or at least I pray it is.

2.

THY KINGDOM COME

'The LORD is my shepherd, I lack nothing.
He makes me lie down in green pastures.'

A psalm of David

It all seemed to happen in slow motion. I came out of the church one sunny spring morning after morning prayers. The birds were singing, the sky was blue and it had rained the day before so the air felt fresh, or as fresh as it can do next to a busy road. A guy of perhaps forty years old or so was huffing and puffing up the hill on a clapped-out old bike – towing a washing machine on some kind of wheeled contraption. The man had his head down as he struggled up the incline, and just as I was about to get into my car, I realised what would come next, which is when everything seemed to slow down. He'd eased off the pedalling as he was coming to the top of the hill, and was at that moment just before the descent, the sweet spot when all his hard work was paying off. Then it happened. I thought to myself: that washing machine is going to overtake him! It did. The machine gathered pace on the

24

other side and the guy went flying. Crash, bang, wallop! It was a moment of pure comedy – or tragedy: I couldn't decide which.

'Fuckin' hell! Ooh me fuckin' back!'

I rushed down as the man was getting back up.

'I've come off me bike, Vicar,' he moaned.

'I know, I can see ye,' I replied, pulling him up off the ground.

'Thanks, Father,' the man said, and undeterred, he got back on and continued his journey. I watched him go, pedalling away with the washing machine trundling after him. He was probably selling it for scrap for a fiver. Where else but Burnley do you see sights like that, I thought to myself. This is as far from God's kingdom and his green pastures as you can imagine.

We have a song that we sing on the stands of Burnley Football Club:

> No one likes us,
> We don't care.
> We are Burnley, super Burnley.
> We are Burnley from the North.

Sums us up perfectly, yet at the same time I do care that it might be how we perceive ourselves. We know others think we're shit, so it's an illustration of this dark humour that's so prevalent, yet there's pride here. There's a resilience you'd be hard-pressed to find outside of these gritty urban estates. Late comedian Les Dawson characterised my parishioners so well with his impression of a northern working-class woman hoisting her large bosom and gossiping over the yard wall with her neighbours. Those women are still around, and they often hold together families that would otherwise be in crisis. They are the lifeblood of many of these communities – stoic stalwarts, whom Dawson paid tribute to with his humour. Women used to talk over the looms in the cotton mills, miming gossip to each other because they couldn't hear themselves over the noise. Burnley, and many other northern towns, have a proud heritage as mill towns where textile manufacturing took place in the nineteenth century, truly amid the dark, Satanic mills. Burnley was built on the mills. It was one of the biggest cotton producers in the world, and saw the manufacturing of things that simply aren't made any more. The Smith & Nephew factory was based in Brierfield Mill, manufacturing denim and spinning cotton into yarn. We had Lambert Haworth based at Finsley Gate and Healey Royd Mills, supplying shoes and slippers to Marks & Spencer. We still have the world's only surviving steam-powered weaving mill, called Queen Street Mill. When the steam energy kicks in, it's a thing of beauty, taking you instantly back into the industrial past, making a cacophony of sounds as the looms are chugging together.

There is also a deep pride here in the coal mines, which were dotted around the town as part of the Burnley Coalfield that surrounds Burnley, Blackburn, Colne and then heads to the Pennine Hills. Nineteen coal seams were exploited during the course of its history, the most significant fault being at Cliviger Valley.

Coal mining began in earnest during the sixteenth and seventeenth centuries, helped by the development of the Leeds–Liverpool Canal. The area suffered a terrible mining disaster at Hapton Valley Colliery in 1962. At the time, the colliery employed almost four hundred men underground. On 22 March, an explosion 750 feet underground killed sixteen men instantly and three more later died in hospital, a date that is remembered with a memorial each year to this day at Burnley Miners' Club. A young boy had been killed in 1855 when entering some of the old workings with a candle for light, and so the seams were known for being 'gassy', but the source of the explosion was never fully identified.

Each year, on that date, those men are remembered, glasses of 'Bene and hot' are raised, where a shot of the French liqueur Benedictine in hot water is drunk as a chaser, a tradition surviving from toasts made in honour of Burnley's soldiers lost during the First World War. I'm told the miners' working men's club gets through a thousand bottles of the stuff a year, and is the world's biggest consumer of the tipple.

In the woods at the bottom of the cemetery, close to the old pit, is an almost-secret memorial garden to the tragedy, and those who lost their lives. A group of local lads known as The Northern Monkeys cleared the woods, and made planters from the hundreds of tyres that had previously been dumped there. The area, which sits on the fringe of the estate, was known as Little Cornwall, because so many of the Cornish miners came north seeking work, and there is a permanent memorial in the cemetery gardens to all the miners who lost their lives.

Those times don't exist here any longer, but this is still a straight-talking community. As we say, you can't bullshit a bullshitter. Truth is told, and if you don't like it then tough shit. There's also no political correctness. There's very little 'wokeness', which isn't necessarily a good thing, but that's how it is. Many of the conversations I am witness to use very 'industrial' language that can often border on the provocative or offensive. I understand what makes this town tick because I've lived in it since I was a very small boy, and I've worked in it and lived around it for so long. It isn't offensive to me but then perhaps I'm used to the way of life here. If you've got a problem, you say something, vociferously. It's no more troubling than anything I've heard on the terraces at my beloved Turf Moor, Burnley FC's football ground. It's also important to say that we're not just a band of foul-mouthed Northerners. There are huge swathes of culture in the North, alongside our unrivalled industrial heritage. Alongside the terraces and streets, there are parks. It is possible to walk outside of my front door with my dogs, and in two minutes to be in the countryside, where I'll see wild deer, herons, Canada geese and the Leeds–Liverpool canal. The landscape here is beautiful, surrounded as it is by the West Yorkshire moors and the glorious view of Pendle Hill, with all its history of witch trials in the seventeenth century. We are close to Manchester, and we're 30 miles from the Costa Del Blackpool, so this is a fabulous place to live.

The core of 'Northern-ness' is unchanging, despite the world around us shifting and evolving. Where there were textile manufacturers, we now have call centres and café culture. There is a huge amount of pride and it is absolutely centred upon each district. We're proudly Lancastrian, but we're clear that we're from Burnley, not Blackpool or Preston, but Burnley. It's like being part of a tribe, but it's also a celebration of us being a unique place. Everybody here wears Claret and Blue, the colours of the football team. If you Google 'Burnley' what comes up straight away is Burnley FC's site. We have an alumni association of people who shout about their pride in this town, such as David Fishwick, who set up Burnley Savings and Loans (BSAL) and published his book *Bank of Dave*, which will one day be a Netflix biopic. He grew up in one of the terraces in a cobbled street and, like most round here, knows what it's like to grow up with nothing. There is also Radio One DJ Jordan North, who rowed from London back home to Burnley upstream on Britain's canals to raise money for Red Nose Day, and there's actor Sir Ian McKellen. Prince Charles championed the restoration of Weavers' Triangle, a derelict area with a huge amount of history that has been renovated by young people from the Prince's Trust. The University of Central Lancaster (UCLan) has a campus here in our town, and is one of the best performing colleges in the country. I've had opportunities to leave Burnley, but who could leave a place that renames a pub The Royal Dyche after the manager of the football club, despite the fact he was sacked? Burnley Football Club is the beating heart of the town and has replaced the community aspect that the Church used to bring. There was massive disappointment at Dyche's sacking because he represented something. He led us to the promised land, and then some more. As a kid growing up in Burnley, I never thought I'd see our beloved club be successful, but I did and I think it was pretty much all down to him. His straight-talking approach to work was something us Burnley folk could relate to. He never buttered things up. He had the approach so many have around here: if you don't like it, then tough shit. That's Burnley FC to a tee that is, and our club will be poorer without him. When famously tall Peter Crouch joined the squad, fans erected a sign above a bridge that read: 'Welcome, Crouchie, mind your head lad.' Where else do you find humour like that, except here?

My first baptism at St Matthew's as a training incumbent involved a delicate situation that really introduced me to the community I was serving. We're quite Catholic in our traditions here, and so the usual congregations are generally from the older community and they dress smartly for church, like they used to do through the centuries. These days, our baptisms often look more like crowds queuing for a night club, and that's how people feel they look their best. To them, it makes perfect sense that looking good is how they want to go out at night. It's not for me to judge them. God doesn't care what we're wearing, though I admit it raises a few eyebrows with the older members of the congregation. On that day, Father Mark, who was the incumbent of St Matthew's at the time, floated into the vestry wearing his cassock.

'Just a word of warning, Father Alex, but the mother of the child in the front row is not wearing any knickers.'

For a moment, I thought I'd misheard him.

'Er, not wearing knickers, Father Mark? But how do you know?'

This wasn't exactly the kind of conversation I expected to have with the priest who was helping me complete my training. I was nervous enough already before the ceremony, one of the sacred rites entering the child into God's grace, without this bombshell.

'Well, she's wearing a very short dress, and when she sits down ...' Father Mark, who is a very exacting, perfectionist man, looked to be in agony as he told me. I think I may have raised an eyebrow but I had no words to reply. I was literally struck dumb, and I was already panicking about where to look during the readings.

'I was in the chapel doing the last checks, and she was just there ...' I felt he was looking to me for guidance.

I took a deep breath. No one had ever said doing this job would be easy. I was about to assist in the first step a child takes in their journey with God, and now rather than focusing on the beauty of this sacred event, I was working out how to try and be as holy as possible.

God was in the proceedings that day. I went out to begin the ceremony and there was the woman in all her glory, but the baby fussed at the font, and so the grandmother passed the child back to its mother, covering her with the christening gown in the process. Meanwhile, I was trying very hard not to get the giggles and to refocus my mind on spiritual matters, which is often hard, I can tell you. Baptisms, or christenings, are a spiritual rite of passage, yet I often wonder how many parents are actually thinking, *Thank God my baby's saved from hell. Thank God my baby has a passage to heaven.* It's sometimes just an excuse for a piss-up. A family turned up for a baptism recently with a full picnic bag. As I was conducting the 15-minute-long ceremony, they were handing out sandwiches, cakes and three-litre bottles of Tizer. Being told there are twenty or more godparents is also not unusual.

'Only six more, Vicar,' I was told by a young couple, Dave and Sam, after listing the seventeenth name.

'Welcome to Burnley, Father,' Father Mark said, grinning.

Another family named one of their godparents as a guy called Mohammed. I had to explain gently that the Church of England does not accept Muslims, however lovely, to be Christian godparents.

I never wanted to be a priest. If I couldn't be a member of eighties' synth band Depeche Mode, then I wanted to be a stand-up comedian or a football referee. Stepping into the pulpit isn't far off the experience of standing on stage about to deliver my first lines, but this time I have God – or, to be more accurate, he has me. I wasn't born up North either. I was made in Tooting in London, but my parents moved up here when I was small and we've been here ever since. I cannot imagine living anywhere else. It is part of my bones, and to be serving as the vicar of St Matthew's is a huge honour. I love this parish, and I love this town. Yet every day, I see those who have been left behind by society, left behind by the wealthy and powerful, and they fall further and further back. Every day, I see opportunity and possibility wasted, I see people who, in other circumstances, may have made something of their lives. I see people who have nothing, literally nothing, except each other. So, I want this book to be part of an awakening, a call to action to make our society better, to fix those most broken, those whom governments and politicians appear to care little for. I want this book to echo the psalm of David and create those idyllic-sounding green pastures, because there aren't too many of those in central Burnley.

It never fails to amaze me that we live in an advanced society with brilliant minds. We created the locomotive steam engine. We created the most successful vaccination drive in history. Yet we cannot solve poverty, and every day more and more people fall through the cracks. Again, it isn't good enough. It isn't acceptable. The Levelling Up agenda has been kicking around up here for a while now, an initiative until recently led by The Rt Honourable Michael Gove MP, the Secretary of State for Levelling Up. The idea behind it, according to the government, is to spread opportunity and prosperity to all parts of the UK, shifting resources to 'Britain's forgotten communities'. What a load of bollocks that is. It's a wonderful aspiration, but I just don't see it happening any time soon in the streets around St Matthew's. Around here, we have rows upon rows of run-down and neglected terraces. Some have made an effort, planting hanging baskets and keeping the front of their modest homes clean, while others have large satellite dishes sitting on the brick frontage, with peeling paint, missing bricks, and weeds growing abundantly on the unkempt path to the front door. When will the people who live in these homes, the ones I walk past every day while taking out my dogs, see the benefits of the Levelling Up agenda? Certainly nothing is changing for these people yet; if anything, their situation looks bleaker now than it did pre-pandemic. Please don't think I'm putting down the homes or people of the estates. I feel as passionately about them and their welfare as I do about the state of the Church and the future of Christianity, as, to me, both fates feel entwined.

I'm not even sure what Levelling Up means. Does it mean that people in the North will get the same opportunities as people down south? Does it mean that people in poverty will be helped to a place of manageability? Well, come on, let's see it then. I want the people in this book to be the ones the difference is made to. These are the people who from the outside look like they live in dangerous terrain, full of pitfalls, fears and problems. They do, of course, but they are also exactly where God has led me over the past few years – and at times, dealing with them has been frightening and difficult. I do it because of my devotion to Jesus, because that is exactly where he would've walked. I think if he was around today, he'd march into Westminster and turn over the tables, just as he did at the temple. He'd walk into our urban estates and gather around him all those who are broken and troubled. He'd fill stadiums with people, and he'd set about sorting it out. And he would be right to do so. When do we tackle these issues of poverty, neglect and aspirational deprivation, if not now? When do we work out what legacy we want to leave our children and grandchildren, if not now?

It is my opinion that we need more disciples. We need more people to get out there and take actions based on Jesus' gospel of loving thy neighbour and caring for the poor. The decline of the Church is deeply distressing to me, but it speaks of a wider apathy towards spiritual matters. Our congregation numbers suffered after the lockdowns as people got used to not coming to the actual church and the habit of attending services got broken. The same thing has happened up and down the country to an already declining attendance, and it makes me wonder how we will survive. At St Matthew's we have been very fortunate in attracting support and donations after the 2020 screening of the documentary *The Cost of Covid: A Year on the Front Line*, but we know we're always in a fragile position. Sometimes, I worry that I will be the last vicar of St Matthew's as there simply won't be churches in every town and village any more.

We carry our own burdens and have to pay in excess of £20,000 to the diocese each year before we can do anything else. There is a belief that the Church of England is wealthy, and that is certainly true for some dioceses that sit on huge wealth and resources, but rarely does that money find the light of day in parishes like Burnley, or Blackpool. Money is tied up in land or buildings, and it isn't easy to move it around because the Church of England is shackled by its own archaic rules and regulations. There are churches that are cash rich, and some that are pretty much destitute, and they are all governed by the Parish Church Councils, making individual decisions about the wealth each church holds. Even the Archbishop of Canterbury, Justin Welby, cannot make a PCC do what he wants them to do.

There are many who are loyal to a tradition that is conservative, evangelical and a traditional Catholic position. What gets lost, for me, comes back to Jesus' word. He gave us a very clear directive, and it is the one I serve and will continue to serve. Working for the state church is a bit like it was working for Woolworths, I imagine; more a case of palliative care being given before it slowly dies out. I hope this isn't true. I know I could walk away but I choose not to because of Jesus' truth.

I hold to a relaxed liberal position, and it is my view that not every story or verse in the Bible is true, but it has wonderful teachings if we care to listen. I'm also aware that I'm a white, heterosexual man and have never suffered the indignity of being attacked for my sexuality or my gender. I have never been told that what and whom I love is wrong, and is sinful and will send me to hell. I cannot imagine how that feels to someone; it is abhorrent to me. It's incredibly difficult to defend an institution that is known to be homophobic, misogynistic and racist. Lord Paul Boateng, a former Labour backbencher, a member of the House of Lords and chair of the Archbishops' Commission on Racism, spoke to us at General Synod recently. He said that racism is a 'gaping wound in the body of Christ'. He said there are people in the Church who believe that homosexuality can be 'healed' or rectified, and these are horrifying statements. The structure of the Church itself is set up to create and maintain such views. Gay clergy can only be ordained into holy orders if they commit to a life of celibacy. The Church separates itself from the secular world, yet it should be one and the same, which is why we must bring about profound change. This is all God's world, and the Church has brushed far too much under the carpet through the years, all of which has been incredibly damaging. Like anything, if an organisation or institution is not built upon integrity and honesty, then it will fail. My whole life has been built upon trying to be a man of truth, and I found a role model in Jesus. Nowhere in the Beatitudes did he say, 'Blessed are those who persecute gay people or women.' Nowhere did he say, 'Blessed are those who make loads of money and don't give a stuff about the poor.' I give thanks to God that I'm not a Christian of indoctrination. I did not grow up having the Bible drummed into me, fearing the dire consequences of not believing. I have received calls from people telling me my views are wrong and I will go to hell, and no doubt, after reading this, I'll receive a few more. The difficulty for me is to ask myself: how can I love a person who holds such entrenched views? I have friends who hold to a conservative theological position and it has been hard, but we have found a place of tolerance and acceptance for each other's views. I want to change the prevailing narrative that the Church is corrupt and bereft of compassion or care, unrepresentative of the people it serves. I want to see the Church of England change dramatically, coming out of its middle-class bubble, its 'Waitrose worship', and actually start to represent who we are as a nation now – a culturally, economically and psychologically different territory from even a hundred years ago. In places where there are high levels of challenge, in Africa and China, Christianity is thriving, whereas here we are struggling outside of the main festivals of Easter, Advent, Harvest, and the usual weddings, baptisms and funerals.

What gives me hope is what we're already doing, which I want to evangelise about in these pages. If we shut down all the church foodbanks, thousands and thousands of people would go hungry. The impact on the country would be huge. Across the UK we have 16,000 churches, 42 cathedrals and thousands of children being educated at our schools, which also fills me with pride. There is good work being done if only we'd recognise it. It is also more than just the outreach work we do; I believe the country is crying out for more Christian awareness, for the teachings of Jesus' gospel. We can say to society, let's be more compassionate. Let's be kinder and more tolerant. As a church, let's stand up for the marginalised, let's speak for the voiceless. Let's look at how drug epidemics are destroying so many communities. Let's focus on whether working families can afford to eat rather than worrying about what celebrities or the royal family are up to. I ask our country's leaders: can you take me to a place in the UK that isn't ravaged by addiction or poverty? It is my view that stories written thousands of years ago can form the heart of a new way of being in our contemporary world, and this gives me hope. Jesus explains that to do God's work, we need to have faith in him, and this gives us the power to be part of the miracle.

Isn't that how we will mend society? Isn't that how we will look at those who have come from a place of privilege and ask more of them, demand they do more for those in spiritual and financial poverty? If the Lord is my shepherd, he is guiding me like one of his flock towards the green pastures that the Levelling Up agenda promises, and only then, perhaps, will we see real change. I'm not political, in that I don't care which party is in power; I just want them to step into the urban estates of the North, or anywhere in this country, and see with their own eyes whom they are meant to be serving. Come to Burnley. Come and see our community, share in our troubles, our resilience, our pride. Come and talk to us about Levelling Up, and tell us what it will mean to those of us here who have to choose between a meal and heating their home. I care for these people, knickers or no knickers.

3.

CALMING THE STORM

'... a time to mourn and a time to dance ...'

Ecclesiastes 3:1, 'There is a time for everything'

Some people think storms never end, but that's not true; all storms have an end, though sometimes it can seem very distant. I have been called to offer comfort and hope many times where perhaps there is little to be had. This is the nature of the work I do, and every day I am reminded that it is impossible to have a perfect life. No one has that, yet we forget and we expect things to go well when the reality is, for many people, that there are big troughs and swells that have to be navigated.

The story of Jesus calming the storm is one of the miracles of his gospel. I told this to a young couple who I'd been asked to visit one rainy day, not long into my ministry. They lived in a humble home, one of the council properties on the estate, with a slightly overgrown patch of grass out the back and peeling paint on the window and door frames. It was small but clean, and I was led into the lounge to sit with them.

'How can I help you?' I asked, sitting on an armchair that was squeezed against the wall underneath a large telly.

The young woman, named Sally, who must only have been in her early twenties, said simply: 'Father Alex, we've had a miscarriage.'

Her partner George was silent and I could see he was close to tears. Clearly a loving couple, they sat holding hands on the sofa as a relative made us all a brew.

'I'm so sorry to hear that,' I said. 'Would you like me to pray for your child?'

They both nodded. Sally had tears rolling down her face now and she looked pale. Both were obviously heart-broken.

I prayed for their lost baby, and asked God to watch over them, much as I did for Mark, hoping it might bring them some comfort. Then, because it felt like the right thing to do, I told them the story of Jesus calming the storm.

'One evening, Jesus was in a boat with his disciples, crossing the Sea of Galilee. Suddenly, storm clouds gathered and the waves began to rise and the boat started to rock. Water washed over the boat, almost swamping it. Storms appeared out of nowhere on this stretch of sea, and the disciples began to panic. Jesus, meanwhile, was asleep on a cushion in the stern, nicely chilled out.

'The disciples woke him in a state of fear and panic, saying: "Teacher, don't you care if we drown?" Jesus calmed the storm, saying: "Peace! Be still!" Miraculously, the seas calmed, the storm died down and the danger passed. Jesus turned to his disciples and asked them: "Why are you so afraid? Do you still have no faith?"

There was a pause after I'd finished and I wondered if it was too much. Sally nodded and glanced at her partner, who shrugged.

'I know life doesn't feel as simple as that story, but it tells us that the storms pass and there is always hope for the future, or at least, that's how I see it,' I added. What I didn't tell them was that I knew exactly how they felt because my wife Sarah and I had been through the same experience many years previously. In the Beatitudes, Jesus says as part of his Sermon on the Mount: 'Blessed are those who mourn, for they shall be comforted.' Those words tell me that actually our pain can be a blessing, and it can bring us closer to God. Our trials make us stronger spiritually, as God blesses the broken and the mourning. Sarah's miscarriage was one of the hardest things I've had to deal with in my life. We met when she was 16 and I was 18 years old. I was working in a small telly shop, and I used to sit and watch the world go by through the window. I remember Sarah and her friend walked past, and so my mate and I followed them to Padiham Road bus stop. We asked them if they fancied going out and the other girl said, 'Alright.' Sarah didn't say a word. She was really quiet, but I discovered she was a mad fan of The Smiths while I was a die-hard fan of Depeche Mode, so I decided that was a good start. We took the under-age girls illegally to a pub, and I remember asking my mate to back off Sarah because I really liked her. She was so pretty, so beautiful – and still is. It was hopeless, of course, yet somehow Sarah didn't run away. She wrote her number on the back of my hand in Biro and I said I'd call her. When I called the number, it rang and rang. I didn't realise but she worked in a chippy on Saturdays and that was the number she'd given me. When the chipper was working they couldn't hear the phone. I kept trying and then decided this was the last time I'd call, and thankfully, she picked up. We have been together ever since, and we now have three children, Joe, 24, Holly, 20, and Rachel, 17, three dogs – Fletcher a cross-collie, and two Patterdale terriers, Jasper and George – plus a cat called Chloe.

At the time of Sarah's miscarriage, comfort felt thin on the ground. Now, I am grateful for the experience as it helps me to connect ever deeper with people such as Sally and George. I left them in a house of silence. No one spoke. No one cried as the stillness of grief was settling upon them.

I use this story a lot in my ministry to offer some hope or comfort to the large numbers of people suffering, or experiencing traumatic situations, and I want them to feel there is a way out, if not today, then perhaps tomorrow.

'Father Alex, me daughter won't go to school and I don't know what to do. What should I do? She just won't go and I'm at the end of my tether.'

The woman standing in front of me was someone I recognised as she'd started to attend church regularly. Until that point, we hadn't spoken. She was a quiet, extremely tired-looking woman who came in with her husband and several of her five children each week. She could've been any age from 30 to 50 years old; her skin was pale, her face gaunt and her mousy-coloured hair was streaked with grey. She was dressed in the seemingly standard outfit of jeans and a sweatshirt, her hair pulled back off her face and with no make-up. From outward appearances, I would've described the family as chaotic. The father didn't appear to be in work and the children appeared apathetic at best, while their mum just seemed exhausted. She looked like someone who only ever just survives, rather than lives and enjoys her life.

'I'm not sure how I can help, but I can listen,' I said, gesturing for her to grab a chair and have a chat.

'The eldest won't go to school. They've tried to make her and so have I, but she just don't want to go.' I felt strangely heartened that this woman wanted her child to attend school, as I see families who really don't give a shit.

'How old is your daughter?' I said, sipping my brew.

'She's fifteen, Father Alex, and she just wants to hang around with her mates and not go to classes. I don't know what to do …'

'She's lucky to have a mum who cares enough for her to want her to go. I don't always see that, so you're already doing something right,' I said by way of encouragement. She gave me a small smile, but even that looked sad.

'But what else is goin' on at home? I don't want to pry, but if ye don't mind tellin' me I'll gladly hear ye out,' I said.

I try and put people at their ease, while also recognising I might be the only non-judgemental person in their life. Everyone has an opinion, don't they? But sometimes people just need to go somewhere and talk without anyone putting their two-penn'orth in or reaching for yet another form to fill in.

'Their dad, well, he has anger problems and he can't keep a job. He's in and out of work, and I think it's that that's affecting the girls. We're skint and it's hard for them, like. And my oldest, well, she has Attention Deficit Disorder or so they say, and she gets bullied at school. They've had to have the police out and everythin'. There's always fights at school and my kids get picked on so she don't want to go no more. I can see why she's strugglin', but I'm worried about her doin' nothing all day; she'll get into trouble if she's bored.' The woman sighed and tried to smile, but her face looked uncomfortable, like she didn't manage to do that much.

'And how are *you* in all this?' I asked.

She shrugged. It's a gesture I see a lot of people make. It seems to me that it's an acknowledgement of the helplessness and powerlessness they feel in their lives, run as they are by benefit claims and being skint all the time, alongside the emotional and mental health conditions so many have.

'Me? I'm alright, Father. I get on but it's hard, like.' I could see it was hard.

'What's your name?' I asked.

'I'm Rosemary, my partner is Ian, and the kids are Mackenzie who's six, Riley who's nine, Elsie who's eleven, and the eldest, Layton and Lucy. We've got a social worker, like ...'

'And does the social worker help at all?' I said.

'Well, not really. Social Services say they want to help us, but we've been with them a few years now and they don't seem to do much. My daughter still won't go in and there seems to be nowt I can do.'

I looked at her, and for a moment I couldn't help but remember my schooldays. Dyslexia wasn't a 'thing' in the 1970s and so mine went undiagnosed throughout my formative years, which meant I had to self-diagnose it and learn to work with it as I got older. Because of this, I found school traumatic and difficult, so I related to the daughter's story in a really personal way. To say I was a bad student would be an understatement. I used to bunk off every Wednesday because of the lessons that day, and I would hide in the school library to try and get out of lessons. Possibly, the most humiliating experience was filing into the library to sit a maths exam, and finding there was no desk with the papers and a pencil laid out for me. My maths was so terrible that I was not even put in for the exams, and I had to go off to another part of the school to join an art lesson. My maths teacher later took me aside one day and told me the only maths I'd ever need was to put on a bet. To this day, when the Grand National happens, I'm your man. So, I knew what this teenage girl might be feeling, or at least I could guess at her reasons for not going to school, but even so, I felt enormous sympathy for the woman sitting next to me who desperately wanted her daughter to better herself, to get an education and make a life for herself. Saying that, Rosemary seemed almost accepting of the situation, and not for the first time I wondered why things had been left to get to this point. Who among the services cared enough to really help them rather than tick the required boxes and say they were trying? No one, it seemed.

Just then, Ian came over. Again, I couldn't have guessed at his age, as his face had the same worn-down look. He was skinny with short hair and stubble. He was scowling, and I could see he wasn't best pleased by his wife having a chat with me.

'Hello, I'm Father Alex, it's good to meet ye,' I said, standing up.

The man shrugged: 'Alright.' Then he looked over to his wife.

'Come on' is all he said and so she threw me another of her not-quite-smiles, called over the three younger children they'd brought with them, and all five of them sloped out. What saddened me most was the feeling that this family didn't experience much joy in their lives. Amid their problems, their burdens, the raging storms, there didn't seem to be a point where the storm ever calmed enough for them to have fun together. Obviously, I'd only just met them and I do not assume I know everything about people. I let them tell me about themselves, which people are surprisingly happy to do once they realise I have no agenda except to listen and support them however I can.

What stood out for me immediately though was that there didn't seem to be anyone who cared enough about these children to set them on a better path. It sounded like they'd been with Social Services for a while, but that there was no real plan, or none the woman seemed aware of. Again, I cannot help but think that the real pandemic is that nobody cares. Nobody cares enough to uncover the root causes of this chaos. Nobody cares enough to find out what is actually going on and make positive changes. Many would argue, rightly, that it is the parents' responsibility to manage their children and get them to school, but what if the parents are themselves lost? What if they were never cared for properly and so do not know how to do the same for their kids?

There is a lovely little boy called Thomas, a six-year-old lad whom I know from one of our schools. He is full of character and fun, a real little character. When I dropped off a food parcel to his mother one hot summer day, he jumped out and squirted her with a water pistol in their small scrap of a garden outside the council flat they lived in. Thinking we would all laugh together at his playfulness, I was shocked by what happened next.

'You fucking little bastard. Do that again and I'll kill you.' His mum swore at him, loudly. His face registered the shock I also felt, and his bubble was well and truly burst. What happened next was worse, though. Once the shock had passed, he shrugged and ran off. It was that same shrug, that almost accepting gesture that I see so often. I came away rattled. Something about the incident upset me deeply. It wasn't so much the bad language, though hearing a small child being lambasted in such a nasty way was horrifying, but it was his response that made me feel a sense of grief. When language like that is normalised in a home, day in, day out, it becomes dangerous for that child and their upbringing. How can they value themselves and be good citizens if what is modelled to them is anger, hostility and language like that? Who is going to teach those children about useful skills and inspiring outcomes if their educators are parents who lack that education themselves?

The teenage children in Rosemary's family are on the pathway of difficulty; that much seems obvious even now as I've watched some of their interactions when they have come into church after I finally spoke to their struggling mum. I know that some people will break the mould and go on to live useful, happy lives, but most don't. Most sink. Most go on to perpetuate the same cycles they were subjected to, and that, to me, is the real poverty I am faced with here. That is the real poverty our politicians must address; that is what our services, law-makers, schools, institutions and law courts must deal with and face. I am deeply concerned that our young people are subjected to environments that are, at times, hostile. I know I have a lot to learn about this family, but looking at Rosemary I get a sense of how things are. She's ragged. She looks exhausted, depressed and defeated. Her shoulders seemed to be permanently drooping, her manner exuded misery and upset. Some people walk around with a big black cloud above them, and that is how I would've described this family that day. It's heartbreaking – and it shouldn't be happening. Children should be joyous, they should be happy and free, rather than drowning in anger and problems.

Growing up, dealing with problems at school and my OCD, I recognise that I wasn't surrounded by the kinds of poverty that I see within that family, and within the parish I serve. I had a loving family and we had enough to live on, so I was able to pull myself through my own troubles. That context simply didn't exist for this family, and so many others like them. I saw poverty of aspiration as attempts to move forward seemed blighted. I saw role-model poverty – and I believe this alone reduces the odds for those siblings. What dumbfounds me is that the plight of this family, and so many like them, cannot be good for society. In many areas of the UK, there are people who will never maximise their potential. There must be skills, talents and dreams that are continually quashed by poverty in one form or another. How does this benefit the community as a whole? I would argue it doesn't at all, so why aren't we fixing it? Why aren't our politicians fighting for these people?

No one has ever believed in them. No one has ever told them they are worth something.

Over the years, I built up a resilience banked from those years of failure at school. I'd built up my character, and it was ingrained within me not to give up. These children, and many like them across the country, go home from school and play *Fortnite*, often until the early hours each night. At the weekend, they do the same. In the school holidays, they do the same. It seems to me that we're missing an opportunity to inspire children, to give them aspirations. For these people the eye of the storm never seems to move away. Sometimes, I despair for the people who just cannot break the cycles of poverty and hopelessness, yet I cannot judge them. I know what it is to fail, to be told you're not good enough, and I know how that feels.

What brings me comfort is that Jesus does not discriminate in his love for people. In today's world where it is a lottery as to who gets what and when, that is a radical statement. Some people say that Jesus was a socialist and that perhaps the root of the socialist ethos connects with his gospel. I'm not so sure, but his gospel is meant to bring good news, that is his message. I am sure of the fact that everyone is equal in God's eyes, and the heart of the gospel is helping each other. This probably means little in the leafy streets of Buckingham or Epsom, but in the urban estates of the UK this is the reality. We have a lot of work to do to make things better, to improve lives, to get to the root causes of the problems of apathy and hopelessness. What depresses me is that I don't think we're any nearer to that happening. I suspect that if I was writing this in a year's time, there'd be a year's worth of new stories to tell about people living with distress and chaos. The numbers coming to our foodbank tell me this is the truth. More and more people come on a weekly basis. These people have poor mental health. They have poor physical health and are exhausted, depressed and struggling to work out how to actually live. It's incredibly sad. We are on a journey at St Matthew's to become a church of outreach, and this is a difficult path. It is hard to see people living grim lives in challenging circumstances. They are just about hanging on. They're not living – they're just about surviving, which might mean avoiding a kicking that day, or paying a bill, or finding the money for the rent or the leccy.

In Burnley, the council has just done up our town hall and created a splendid pedestrianised street in a local suburb, at considerable expense. It's wonderful, but to me it seems like we're papering over the cracks, portraying an image of well-being when you don't have to dig very deep to find real hardship, and absolute poverty. What are our priorities here? Making a town pretty or helping its residents? The wounds of northern towns such as Burnley, Rochdale and Blackburn lie near the surface, if only we would look.

Storms seem to be constantly on the horizon. A guy came in to church the other day, and I actually felt quite scared. He came in half an hour before the service, so I was alone, opening up the church. He wore a balaclava and a backpack, which can sometimes be what heroin addicts carry with their equipment for shooting up inside. I couldn't see his face but he was shaking and sweating. My first instinct was that he was going to attack me. This doesn't happen often, but when it does I become acutely aware that I am alone in the church, and things can get very scary indeed. Instead, the man went off on one.

'Father, I need to tell ye. There isn't just one God, there are lots of gods, there are loads,' he said, tripping over his words in his haste to get them out. I looked over at the door, which, thankfully, was open, in case I had to do a runner.

'Okay, how do ye work that one out?' I said, hoping to engage him in a chat.

His clothes didn't look very clean and he smelled a bit, like he was sleeping rough. I don't judge anyone for their appearance. I am here to embrace everyone, regardless of their social standing or financial position, but at times like this I'm also wondering if I'm safe or not.

With shaking hands, he pulled a Bible out of his pocket, and shouted suddenly: 'Do you remember me? Do you remember me?'

I was frightened, but I managed to reply as calmly as I could: 'I don't know, mate. You'll need to take the balaclava off as I can't see you.'

The guy hesitated for a moment, then he dipped his head down and pulled the black woollen thing off his head. He must've been warm as it was a mild day, but I also sensed that he was coming off something or having a mental health crisis as he was trembling, and his speech was slightly slurred.

'Oh, it's you. Yes, I remember ye,' I said, smiling now, though the fear hadn't entirely dissipated. It was a man called Gary who had been in and out of the church for a while, then vanished as many people do. Goodness knows what he'd been up to in that time, but he looked in a bad way. I was in the middle of getting ready for a morning service so I kept walking, checking hymn books and making sure everything was ready. I felt grateful that within five or ten minutes people would start arriving and I wouldn't be alone. As I walked, Gary was behind me, following me around the church, speaking in an urgent, staccato way as if this was extremely important. From the corner of my eye, I saw the Bible in his hand as he kept gesticulating, and I wondered if he was going to thump me with it.

'But there are many gods, Father, do ye see?' He kept repeating himself, and I realised he probably wanted reassurance from me that it was okay to think this, which of course was up to him. My belief is different, but that doesn't stop me from acknowledging his understanding.

'Come and sit down,' I said at last, and pointed at a couple of chairs closest to the altar. I closed my eyes for a moment and breathed.

'My belief is that there is one God, and his Son, Jesus Christ, came to earth to save us from our sins. I follow Jesus and that's what I believe to be true. What you believe is entirely up to you. If there are many gods, then that's your belief. Why don't you stay for the service? It might help ...'

Gary was looking around the church, still agitated, but he nodded.

'Alright, Father Alex.'

The congregation arrived and Gary stayed seated at the front. The service started, but as soon as I began, his voice kept sounding.

'But Father Alex, there are many gods.'

I continued.

'But Father Alex, isn't it true there is more than one god?' Gary interrupted again, this time holding up his small battered-looking Bible. I had to do something. I could see members of the congregation looking over at him, distracted and getting a bit miffed by his interjections.

'Now then, brother, you need to shut up now; we can continue this chat afterwards.'

'Alright, Father, alright,' Gary mumbled, shifting in his seat, his agitation appearing to increase. I carried on, though I was wondering what might come next.

'Let us pray. Our Father, which art in Heaven, hallowed be thy name ...' I started the Lord's Prayer and I saw something change in Gary. He seemed to settle down. He was mouthing the words, and already I could see his nervous energy change a little.

'For thine is the Kingdom, the power and the glory. For ever and ever. Amen.'

Gary stood up when we finished, and not bothering that he was addressing me as I led the service, he added in a typical Lancastrian way: 'I'll see ye in a bit.'

It seemed to me that Gary's storm was calmed even in the few minutes he stayed and listened.

Right now, it feels as though we, as a country, are in the eye of a perfect storm. First, we had Brexit. Then a global pandemic and lockdowns. Then, conflict in Ukraine and the cost-of-living crisis. It feels like we're on a precipice, and we don't know which way to turn. I believe it's a good thing to make a bob or two, and enjoy nice holidays, but I also believe that those people who are in a better position have a duty to look after those who are less fortunate. I recognise over the past few years that St Matthew's has become a place of sanctuary for many. It is also a place of hope and inspiration, joy and fun. The church has become a bridge between prosperity and austerity, a safe haven for people, and that's a really good thing. What I want to see changed is how the system itself works. It's no use having a system of left versus right, where each side has to vote against the opposing side. Surely, what our country needs is a new way of doing things, a way that means we all sit around a table and work together to improve people's lives. I genuinely believe we have lost the ability to discuss problems and resolve them rather than fight and squabble. I have thought about putting myself forward to become an MP, but I couldn't buy into all that bullshit. Underneath all this, all the storms, all the damaged people, all the sorrow, sadness and joy I see on a daily basis, for me it always comes back to God. I calm my own storms through my faith in Jesus, through his teachings and the beautiful words of the liturgy. Jesus implied that what those disciples caught out in a boat during a storm needed was faith. I'm not sure that's true: faith doesn't stop bad things happening, but what it does is give us back some oars, so that we can carry on rowing, carry on through stormy waters until we reach the safety of the shore.

4.

JENNY SWEARS-A-LOT

'Have I not commanded you? Be strong and courageous.
Do not be afraid; do not be discouraged, for the Lord
your God will be with you wherever you go.'

Joshua 1:9

Jenny is as Burnley as they come. She's ballsy, brash and
straight-talking, and she doesn't give a shit what anybody else
thinks. Every second word is a swear word, normally an
f-bomb, which is why I've given her the name Jenny Swears-
a-Lot in my phone. I really like her. She is a matriarch in the
strong Lancastrian tradition of women like Ena Sharples, a
character in *Coronation Street*. Jenny doesn't wear a hairnet,
nor does she spend her time gossiping about others, but the
strength of spirit and her determination to protect her family
are unquenchable. Her northern self-sufficient character is not
dissimilar to Ena's at all. Whenever I ask her how she is, she
always replies: 'I'll be rait' (I'll be right). No matter what life
throws at her, no matter how little support she gets, she'll
always get through.

I met Jenny at a ladies' anxiety support group, which was held weekly in a grim-looking 1970s community hall on the Stoops estate. The estate is famous – or infamous – for the Burnley Riots of the 1990s and then again in 2001, when the streets around the area erupted into a night of violence. Cars were cremated and left in black mangled heaps on the road-sides while shopfronts and houses had their windows smashed, pubs were petrol-bombed and people fought on the streets. Businesses, and livelihoods, went up in flames, as people vented their rage at the high levels of unemployment, the deprivation, and the 'us and them' mentality of the white and Asian communities, which was fanned by the rise of far-right-wing movements at the time. The estate doesn't have as many burnt-out cars now, but parts of it were still a sorry sight to behold as I walked towards the community centre on a bleak November day. Broken glass and rubbish were strewn on the large patch of land where the centre is sited, along with evidence of kids using it as a motorcross practice route. If you think of the programme *Shameless*, and the book and film *Kes*, then you'll have a pretty good picture of the area. Actually, the writer of *Shameless*, Paul Abbott, grew up in Burnley, and even though the series was set in an estate in Manchester, he has spoken about the social deprivation of living in the Stoops area in the 1970s. I reached the hall, a dark shuttered building that looked as unwelcoming as it was possible to be. Once inside, everything changed. I sensed immediately that the place was full of love and real support for the women of the estate.

Jenny walked in and plonked herself down. She was wearing trainers, leggings and a sweatshirt. She looked every inch a woman from the working classes, a full-bodied, short-haired, full-of-life character.

'Alright, how are ye?' I asked, expecting the usual polite response that people give when they see my dog collar. Not from Jenny.

'I'm fuckin' shit, how d'ye think I am?' she replied.

As soon as I heard that, I thought, *Ey up, here's someone I'd like to get to know.* Many people treat me like I'm a very pious, sensitive soul and perhaps that's true to some extent, but I prefer it when people are themselves, because it inspires me to be the same. Even people round here tend to apologise if they swear while they're chatting to me, but Jenny couldn't care less. In that room full of women, she really stood out, particularly when we heard what she was up against.

'I've got five kids and three are autistic,' she began, matter-of-factly. 'My fourteen-year-old daughter's been self-harming. She started off with razors, and when we removed them all we thought that was that. Then it carried on.'

There was a moment's silence as everyone took this in.

'How does she self-harm?' someone asked.

'She does it on her legs. She slices herself, with anything. When you think you've got everything, there's something else she uses. Honestly, we've found loads of stuff. I just thought it'd be razor blades, so I had no idea before this started what could be used. She scratches herself to death with my sewing needles, so I've no sewing kit now.

'Then there's cans of pop – she opens cans of pop and unravels them and it's like a long blade then. She drinks these monster cans and she'll open the top and she must just slice round. It's like a long orange peel, and she cuts herself with that. Then there's glass; practically anything you can cut yourself with, she'll find a way. Before you come across it, you think they must just use razor blades; that's what I thought. It wasn't until we removed them and it were still there, you think what the hell's she cutting herself with? They'll break stuff to make it sharp.

'She tried to commit suicide recently. I found her and so I took her to A&E, where we waited for hours; then a nurse came and told us there was no mental health support available, so she gave me a fuckin' leaflet. She said the waiting list for crisis support was fourteen fuckin' weeks. What the fuck am I supposed to do with a fucking leaflet?'

Jenny looked around the room as if any of us could answer that question. Some of the women shook their heads, others muttered in agreement, no doubt having experienced similar situations. I felt deeply shocked.

'Did ye get any help for her in the end?' I said.

'Yeah, she's under help now. She's seeing a psychologist at the minute but she only sees them once a month. It's like a talking therapy thing,' Jenny replied and shrugged.

'And does it help her?' I asked, hoping someone somewhere was doing something for this family. Again, the shrug before replying.

'Erm, I don't know because I don't know what's said in the meetings, which is fair enough, but she don't seem to be any different. She still self-harms ...'

'Outside the talking therapy, is there anything else supporting her? Or is that the only treatment she's getting?'

Jenny looked surprised I would even think there was more support out there.

'That's all she's gettin',' she replied simply.

'And, do you think that's enough?' I couldn't help but ask. I felt like she'd been short-changed but perhaps this woman, who must've only been in her late thirties or early forties, felt differently.

'I don't know.' Jenny looked at me and shook her head. 'I don't know if my daughter Kelly is open with them. She's got autism anyway, and she can't regulate her emotions so she doesn't care what other people think. She'll literally just stare you out. She's probably taking some of it in but you can't work her out. She's a loner, and spends a lot of time with her own thoughts, and it's her own thoughts that tell her to self-harm.'

'And this is on top of your other kids,' said one of the other mums, another knackered-looking lady wearing a hoodie, leggings and trainers.

'Yeah, that's just one of them,' Jenny replied. 'I've got a seventeen-year-old daughter, the bat-shit crazy one who's self-harming, a thirteen-year-old daughter who's fine, just a bit mouthy, a ten-year-old boy and a three-year-old boy. Both boys are also autistic as well.'

'How do you cope?' I asked, bowled over by Jenny's ability to keep going.

'You've just got to fuckin' get on with it. You just carry on. As soon as you stop to think about things, that's when they're overwhelming. It's tough on my relationship, on us both. And it's taken its toll on my husband's mental health. He has to worry every month to get enough money to pay the bills and mortgage. Sometimes, it's harder for men. I worry about him and everyone. People can only take so much, can't they?'

There's something about the northern, working-class sense of responsibility that strikes me whenever I think back to that conversation with Jenny. There is a huge sense of duty to family, to paying bills, to keeping going, which I admire so much. In some ways, I related to Jenny's struggles because I might've been standing there as a priest, but my path to priestdom wasn't an easy one at all, and it took me a long time to discover what I was truly meant to do with my life. Jenny impressed me because she knew absolutely who she was, and she was comfortable with herself in a way I have never really been. I also knew what it was like to be clobbered by life, literally, when I had a short-lived experience as a football referee. I'm passionate about football, yet I failed the first time I tried to become a Class One Ref. At the time, I was devastated, but I tried again and passed the second time around. In some ways, I feel like my whole life has been about 'second time round'. My burgeoning footie career was brought to an abrupt end when a disgruntled player, to whom I'd given a red card during one particularly fraught local match, punched me in the face, knocking me spark out. To 'bring me round' the rest of the team threw a bucket of ice-cold water on top of me for good measure, and it was at that point that my ambitions changed direction away from football. I was also an aspiring comedian, though I hadn't got very far with it despite nights spent scribbling away creating sketches and jokes. Instead, realising the footballing world wasn't ready for me I embarked upon a career in retail with Argos.

After the session, I chatted to Jenny and invited her to come along to the church for a chat and a brew, hoping she would actually come. Jenny agreed but only if her mate came with her. I really like the way the estate women do that. It's a case of 'will do if you do' and it shows the depth of their friendships and the camaraderie that are integral parts of the estate communities, and are their great strength. She went on to say that she and her family live in Burnley Wood, a place where mills, factories and densely populated terraced housing sprang up in the second half of the nineteenth century. Some parts of the area remain affluent, with large stone houses built for the wealthy mill and mine owners, and then there's Jenny's part, an area now blighted by its fair share of drugs and crime. Drug dealing is done openly. It was worse before the alley gates were erected on her back street as it was there that sex workers used to work in cars during the day. Jenny added: 'I'd go outside and think, "For God's sake, she's gettin' a tenner for that …"' On the back street there were one woman who was pregnant, and out doing the bins. We heard noises and thought she'd gone into labour on the back street, or something. My husband went out. It wasn't her but instead there was an old man in a car going for it. It was only 5pm and the kids could've been playing out there as it was summer and still daylight. Literally, that bloke washed his willy with a baby wipe and dropped it on the floor and the prostitute wandered off. I was ringing the police, grassing on them with their registration plates.'

Many of the women nodded as Jenny spoke. It was obvious that witnessing criminal activity was a normal, everyday occurrence. Not for the first time, I asked myself, how on earth can you keep kids from straying off the right path in a place where crimes are committed in broad daylight, and seemingly with impunity?

If I walked out of the vicarage now, it wouldn't take long before I saw criminal activity in some form or another; in fact I know at least one sex worker who sometimes comes to the foodbank. It's endemic everywhere these days, it seems, along with drugs. I only have to stick my head out the window and

I can smell dope. Smelling dope is just normal now, drifting on the night breeze. The fragrance of cannabis is everywhere. People walk down the street with a big joint now whereas years ago you'd expect the police to do something so that people wouldn't be so blatant. It's become normalised, and this worries me deeply. How easy it is for young people to fall into recreational drug use and whatever else follows. Even at the church, we hear stories about it being in school playgrounds; meanwhile anti-social behaviour has gone through the roof. Yet amid the social problems and poverty, women like Jenny keep getting up each day and carrying on. That to me is a miracle.

Other women are completely inspiring and they're lucky enough to live perfectly normal lives and have good strong loving families. I met Julie after I received a call from an undertaker. The call came just after Christmas, and almost knocked me flying.

'Is that Father Alex?' said the voice.

'It is, how can I help?' I replied, one eye on the telly as it was showing some of the classic comedy I love.

'It's the undertaker. It's a tricky one, this one, Alex. It's a young woman who fell down the stairs on Christmas Day and died.'

'Alright, thanks mate. Give me the address and I'll go over today.'

Instantly, all thoughts of TV comedy evaporated, just like my comedy career had done so many years previously, and, instead, I had a sinking feeling. This was not going to be an easy one. In some ways it was a priest's worst-case scenario, a young person in the prime of their life dying in a tragic accident at Christmas. All funerals are sad and tragic in their own way, but some are trickier than others, and this one definitely felt like it might be a difficult journey.

I went to get changed, put on the white strip that gives me such privileged access to the lives – and the griefs – of my community. On the day most associated with celebration and family, a mother had become a grieving mum and I wanted to do right by her. While her late daughter Leigh had lived in the Coronation Street-terraced streets locally, Julie lived in a leafier part of the town, right on the edge of the parish. I drove over and knocked on the door. She lived in a terraced house but it was bigger, and in a better state, than many of the houses around my church. A well-presented professional woman opened the door and introduced herself as Julie, Leigh's mother. No amount of training can prepare a priest for that moment, for walking through a door to meet a recently bereaved family.

'I'm really sorry I have to be here at all. I'm so sorry for your loss,' I said as I stepped inside. Julie led me into her lounge where members of her family were sitting in the pleasant surroundings. It's always hard to know what to say, but at the same time I'm aware that things have to be moved on, for the family to grieve properly.

'Do you want to tell me what happened?' I began, sipping the tea Julie had bought out of the kitchen for me. I never refuse a brew; it's always an ice-breaker when I first arrive anywhere.

'My daughter was settled, and in a happy relationship. We were expecting her to come for Christmas Day dinner at 12pm. She was often late so we didn't worry too much when she didn't show up. Then there was a knock at the door.' My heart sank as I knew what might be coming next. I felt it in my stomach, and I couldn't imagine how this polite, nice woman must've felt.

'Two police officers were at my door. They told me Leigh had had an accident at home that morning, and was in hospital. They told us we needed to be there because she was gravely ill. She'd fallen down the stairs on Christmas Eve, hitting her head. The police took us to her bedside, and I sat with her while she passed away ...'

I nodded. The room was quiet. There were sounds from the park opposite the house, of people walking or dogs and children playing, but the house was silent.

'I'm sorry to hear that, Julie; that must've been a terrible shock,' I said gently.

'It was, Father Alex, it still is. It was Christmas Day of all days.'

We both went quiet. I could sense that Julie might want to come to St Matthew's and see where I was based, so I invited her. A few days later, she came, and when she walked in I saw her face change. She seemed lighter. She smiled as she looked around, then came up to me, and said something I will never forget.

'Father Alex, I knew as soon as I met you that you were the right person to take the service for my daughter's funeral. I can tell you're a safe pair of hands.'

That was honour and praise indeed. The funeral took place, and I've since taken the services of other members of Julie's family, which has also been a huge honour.

Julie has since become a valued member of our church community, and attends services regularly. She would probably say that St Matthew's was a place she felt close to her daughter and it has been a safe sanctuary to reflect upon her loss, so much so that Julie helps teach Sunday school, is involved in setting up our fantastic toddler group, and is a foundation governor at our church school. Julie is a very strong yet modest and quiet lady, who goes about her business with humility and honesty. Christmas Day will forever be a memorial to her daughter, yet she is undaunted and she carries on. As Jenny says, you have to. These women inspire me. They show what happens if you're dealt a different hand, particularly if you're someone who doesn't have buckets of money to soften the blow. For many, having £50 in the bank might mean a chippy tea or a bit of respite going to the pictures, but many don't have the means for luxuries like that. The other day, I gave someone a £4 voucher for the Food Pantry, which is a new service we're supporting. For £5 annual membership and paying £4 a shop, people can choose four items of fruit and veg, seven shelf items and one freezer item, meaning they get roughly £20 worth of food. You'd have thought I'd given this woman the keys to the palace, she was so chuffed to receive the voucher. Most people are authentic. They have an integrity that I just don't see in politicians, and they see straight through any half-hearted efforts to help. They put up with a lot though.

My favourite song is 'Walking in my Shoes' by Depeche Mode, and I attribute those lyrics to all the women I know here in Burnley, and all the people in my parish. It's easy to look at these people from our leafy streets, with our 4×4 cars and our nice clothes and judge them and their lifestyles, but I defy anyone to try walking in their shoes. We would absolutely stumble if we had to face even a moment of what Jenny faces each day. I worry because they are just so weary with it, you can see that in their faces and in the drop of their shoulders.

There are a lot of weary women and weary children in this parish. There are children who have been pulled out of mainstream education, and so they haven't even climbed the first rung in life. What will become of them? At some community events, I've heard kids ask for 'coffee three' instead of a milkshake or a fresh orange. When they've been asked what they mean, they reply, 'coffee with three sugars'. This is kids as young as four or five years old. Coffee is cheap so mothers are giving their kids the drink instead of juice. This says something about how the children here are growing up, with the weariness of the adult world somehow already on their shoulders. The women in my parish, and particularly those in the anxiety group where I met Jenny, absolutely live out Joshua's call to be strong and courageous. They live it and breathe it every day with extraordinary examples of stoicism, resilience and nerves of steel to make it through the shit storm that is their lives. In many ways, they are the perfect examples to me of being steadfast in faith, to truck on in times of adversity. That verse in Joshua tells us, whether we've got problems in our marriages, are going through illness, divorce or bereavement, whether we're facing tough decisions, just to keep going. It can be enough just to put one foot in front of the other some days, and Joshua tells us that challenges will keep coming but we must have courage as God is by our side through it all. This is a verse about endurance, and nowhere is there more of that than on some of our urban estates. Sometimes when I hit the buffers in my ministry, I draw on the Jennys of this world. If she can keep going through the trauma and grief of her experiences then I can model such behaviour, and keep going whenever I feel overwhelmed by the responsibility of caring for my congregation.

5.

LOVE

'Love the Lord your God with all your heart
and with all your soul and with all your mind
and with all your strength ... Love your
neighbour as yourself. There is no
commandment greater than these.'

Mark 12:30–31 NIV

Jenny walked into the church, just as she'd promised to do, with a mate of hers, another stalwart mum from the estate called Judy, an extremely kind-hearted and rather glamorous-looking mum of ten children with bleached blonde hair. I already knew Judy as she often attended church events. It was raining and cold but I'd made sure we had nice biscuits to share while we chatted. I'd thought things were bleak for Jenny, but it wasn't long before I realised I didn't know the half of it.

'What's to do? How are ye? Are ye alright?' I said, beaming at Jenny and Judy. Judy was the matriarch of her large family and I knew her well enough to have a laugh with her.

'Yeah, alright, Alex,' Jenny replied. Judy smiled and sat herself down.

'I'll get you both a brew,' I said, and came back with a mug of tea for each of them.

'Come on, are ye really alright?' I said, sipping the scalding-hot drink.

Jenny and Judy glanced at each other, and it struck me there was as much resignation in their gaze as there was humour.

'Am I fuck, Father!' Jenny sighed.

'What's to do?' I asked in my usual way.

'It's my littlest boy, Arthur. He's got severe autism, like, and he needs a special buggy because he don't have no spatial awareness and he falls over kerbs and keeps hurtin' himself.'

'I'm sorry to hear that, Jenny. And do ye have to buy the buggy?' I said, wondering again at the courage of this woman who seemed to have every challenge possible as a mother.

'They're expensive so we can't afford to buy one. The NHS said it'd take eight weeks to get one, but it's been fourteen fuckin' weeks now and we're still waiting ...' We all sat in silence for a moment.

'I keep asking,' continued Jenny, 'but they say there are delays and what-not.'

'How do you cope?' I said, forgetting about my tea. Sometimes, I simply didn't know how people got out of bed each morning and carried on. Jenny was one of those people, yet here she was in all her wonderful, forthright glory.

'You fuckin' have to, don't ye?' cut in Judy, who smiled, as if there was simply no other way.

'So, I'm guessing you're living on a pretty tight budget?' I didn't want to pry too much, but I knew things weren't easy financially for either woman. Jenny shrugged. That familiar gesture that means 'we take it on the chin'.

'Everything has to be thought about. I'm not proper poor, I do have luxuries, but everything needs to be accounted for. I can't kit my kid out with trainers as I've got three school uniforms to buy, so I put so-much away every month cos that's going to be well over three hundred quid, isn't it, if not more. That's what I do. I sieve a bit away so it's not a massive chunk when I have to buy something.

'I get a big bag of rice or pasta so it's big pan out, and chuck it in, job done.'

'Fair enough,' I replied, marvelling at her straight-forward, no bullshit approach to life. If only Jenny ran the country.

'It's the same for me. I make sure there's enough for every-body, but it isn't posh meals, it's good, basic stuff that fills everyone up. It is what it is,' Judy added, and she shrugged too.

I hear the words 'it is what it is' a lot around here, and accepting our situations is great, but sometimes I want to push people, to ask them if they want more from their lives.

Just then, one of the older members of our congregation, who has probably been a member of the church for forty years or more, walked in.

'Hello, Father Alex,' she said after taking off her wet coat, and making sure she didn't drip rain onto the polished floor.

'Hello, Doris, how are ye? Are ye alright?' Instantly, Doris's hearing aid started screeching.

'Yes, Father, thank you for asking,' she said, completely oblivious to the racket she was making. Behind me, I heard Jenny and Judy giggle.

'I'm going to do a bit of cleaning, don't mind me,' she added, hearing aid still sounding loudly. I sighed. Sometimes our services were more a cacophony of dodgy hearing aids than the angelic voices of the congregation. It came with the fact we had an ageing church population. Some of them had digestive challenges, and found the part where they kneel for Holy Communion, to accept the body and blood of Christ, impossible without farting loudly. How do I keep a straight face? It's really bloody hard, I can tell you.

Women like Doris have been the absolute heart of this church and long may they continue, screeching or not. We have members of the congregation in their eighties and even nineties who care for this place as if it were their own home. They come in and arrange flowers, sort the Bibles and generally make the place beautiful. People like Doris are the heart of St Matthew's.

Jenny and Judy were now chatting to each other as Doris walked off and the sound of her hearing aid became fainter.

'Sorry, Jenny, go on, if ye want to,' I said. My tea had gone cold but it didn't matter in the slightest because conversations like the one we were having are the heart of my ministry. They are the reason I became a priest, because I feel like I'm creating a space to listen and to really hear people in a way perhaps they haven't been heard in their lives. That space is where questions about spirituality and about the presence of God might begin to take place, but I never force that conversation on people. It's enough for me to listen, if I can do nothing else to help. I hope that's what I do anyway. I do drink a lot of tea and eat more biscuits than my waistline can take.

'So, Jenny, has anybody ever asked if you need help, mentally, with everything you're dealing with?'

'Not really, though I go to the anxiety support group. I think parents get shoved under t'carpet, don't they?' she replied.

'Don't take this the wrong way, but your children's issues become your problem because you're their mum. So, what is there for you, supporting you?' I went on.

'I don't know of anything. I've done a few mental health courses, and there's the autism and behavioural courses to understand how to help my kids. Honestly, I don't know if they can help. The doctor just gives me lip service. My daughter who self-harms has started going to a group for gay and trans kids and she seems to like that.'

'When did she come out as gay?' I asked.

'When she were about twelve she come out as bisexual, then for ages she just had girlfriends. She's with a boy now. It don't matter to us what the hell she is,' Jenny said, stoutly.

'It's quite a lot to deal with, I imagine. She's autistic, she's self-harming and she's in a relationship. I want to know how this affects you?' I hoped I wasn't crossing any lines though instinctively I knew Jenny was happy to speak to me so frankly. I don't take this for granted. This is sacred ground, and I would never want Jenny or anyone to feel I was prying into their personal lives.

'I'm alright with everything, really.' Jenny shrugged. She looked at Judy and they shared a glance that somehow spoke of their troubles, yet there was no self-pity there, again just acceptance of their lives.

'You're a survivor,' I said, smiling. 'Can I get you both another brew? Mine's gone cold.'

'It is what it is, isn't it? There's nothing you can do about it. I put my daughter on t'pill as I can't be arsed with grandkids. Luckily, her boyfriend's a proper nice lad. She'll be rait when she's worked herself out,' Jenny added.

Like so many others around here, Jenny lives if not on the edge, then not far off it, at the mercy of NHS waiting lists and benefit payments, yet her love for her kids and her family is what seemed to keep her going. Already, I had a sense that she would fight to the death for her kids, and that was her shining light.

It also seemed to me that it's a life that can keep going until some kind of tragedy or problem hits, after which it might look very different; precarious and unsteady. When my attempt to carve out a career as a football referee ended so brutally, I climbed the ranks at Argos, the large retail chain on the high street. I became a store manager, and ended up running a multi-million-pound outlet and training others to take on roles with the company. What those days as a manager taught me were that resilience is something that we discover in ourselves when we're wading through shit, and love is always the driving force behind that, whether we love our families enough to keep working, whether we love our colleagues or co-workers enough to be the best manager you can be, whether it's our kids and fighting for their rights and their needs to be met, it's always love that underlies everything.

Jenny is already one of the most resilient people I know, and she's learnt it the hard way.

'You're a fucking wanker' was something I heard a lot when I worked at Argos in the heat of a dispute over an electric blanket refund, or an impotent bouncy castle. Apparently, many disgruntled customers 'knew where I lived' or wanted to kill me over the Argos refund policy. I'm immune to bad language after years in retail management and my refereeing 'career'. Actually, I'm really grateful that I have life experience, which means I don't judge or blame people because I've seen and heard it all before. When I see people in certain congregations for weddings and baptisms whom I used to catch shoplifting back in my Argos days, I just smile inwardly.

We had a management tool called Root Cause Analysis (RCA). This was an improvement plan put in place to make a situation better, for example a failing store, or difficulties with staff. Progress was measured over time, and the plans were adjusted accordingly, based on what worked and what didn't. Sometimes I wonder if the things I learnt running large retail stores wouldn't actually be really handy in helping the people of my parish. There are multiple services engaging with people, yet I struggle at times to see any changes to parishioners' lives as a result. People such as Jenny, who has accessed some support, yet her circumstances stay resolutely the same in their complexity and difficulty. By looking at RCA, if progress isn't being made, then more questions have to be asked, more decisions made and improvements suggested. If they're not, what does that say? It says, no one cares enough. It says that we are okay to leave people floundering. Things weren't always done in ways that I felt worked to improve matters.

Key Performance Indicators (KPIs) don't exist in the Church, and I'm really grateful for that. The bottom line of such indicators was financial. Was the store making money? Were employees doing things right all the time? If not, why not? At Argos I had to sack people. Because of KPIs. I once had to follow the line of the Argos law and sack someone who had taken £3 from the till to get a bus home. I knew she had no money because she was skint – she'd told me – but the regulations clearly stated that theft was theft, no matter how small. That nearly broke me as I knew she was struggling. It was a very black-and-white world, and I don't think the Church should be somewhere that operates like that. I was in the harsh competitive world of retail for 20 years, and I have been able to take the best bits from that experience, and leave behind the rest. Argos was full of female leaders, and a significant number of directors were women at the time as well. Female leadership was normal, as it should be, and I never even gave it any thought until I came to the Church and saw that women are still not fully recognised by some as people of leadership and influence.

I often wonder if Root Cause Analysis should be applied to the Church of England itself. The state church is going through a crisis both of identity and inclusion, and perhaps if we understood better where many of the entrenched views about homosexuality, women clergy and different races came from, and why they have flourished, we might become a church with relevance to more people, and to the contemporary world.

Often, I feel forced to ask what relevance the Church and Christianity have to anybody these days, especially those who don't fit into the Songs of Praise, white-middle-class mould that has for so long represented the majority of the Church of England's community. What happens if we're poor, marginalised, queer or black? What then? Does the Church love us all equally? Sadly, it probably does not. Do we have a place inside our state religion if we are someone who doesn't fit that traditional small mould? I argue fervently that, yes, we all should have a place, though the Church itself is bitterly divided over issues of same-sex relationships both within the priesthood and without, and the role of women. I argue that these issues are outdated and we, as a church, must step forward into the contemporary world, extending a warm and real welcome to those who love another of the same gender. In my ministry, I want to feel that women like Jenny, who are navigating the complexities of contemporary relationships and identities like those her daughter is dealing with, can freely and openly trust the clergy to listen without judgement. I want anyone facing questions about their own sexuality or gender to be able to walk into any one of our churches and feel welcome.

Yet, it is still the case that gay priests must renounce loving physical intimacy with their partners in order to fulfil their role. It is still the case that many feel women should not be priests and should not be able to celebrate Holy Communion. For all the welcoming messages, there is a deeply painful wound at the heart of the Church of England that, in my view, will ultimately decide whether it will survive as a church at all.

I am a priest seeking inclusion for everybody, which is surely an absolute basic act of love, and I'm so grateful for my life experiences that give me this view. As a manager at Argos, one of my employees was gay and we became good friends. Occasionally, we'd go out and he'd take me to one of the bars he frequented, and I found the whole experience colourful, entertaining and bright. I never once felt uncomfortable in that environment. Yet this is still a massive political football in the Church, the issue of whether we 'accept' same-sex relationships. My journey of inclusion and believing in an inclusive agenda has come to the forefront of my work within the Church, especially in the General Synod. I want people to feel welcome in the way Jesus wanted us to be: whole-heartedly, and for their unique gifts to be recognised and used in the service of God.

Eighteen months ago, my parish joined the Inclusive Church Network, which is a group of Christian churches that affirm and welcome people of all persuasions and backgrounds, whether that be gay, straight, disabled, black, marginalised, whatever. I'm appalled that gay men and women, black people, people of colour or working-class people might feel unwelcome in our churches. Jesus tells us to serve, and if, by marginalising people from different backgrounds, we're failing to do that, then the Church is in a state of disrepute. From my own perspective, from a place of educational exclusion and frailty, I know how that feels. Let's not use our discrimination to put people down or leave them out; as a Christian that makes no sense to me. This was the driving force behind my decision to stand for General Synod, to be a liberal voice who speaks on behalf of the voiceless. In my election address, I said that I am here to speak on behalf of the silent voices, the people on the fringes of society. I was very clear that I support same-sex relationships, just so there was no ambiguity at all! I was overwhelmingly voted in by the clergy of the diocese, so I am not alone in thinking this – and there have been many championing the cause for much longer than I have. There is hope yet that love will overcome the divisions. I will not be silenced, though, in speaking what I believe is the gospel of Jesus. It is no different from the work we are doing at St Matthew's with our foodbank, our Breakfast Club (which feeds the neediest of the parish), and the work we are doing supporting people with mental health challenges. I am trying to be a voice for the marginalised. I see people every day who feel ignored by the services that are meant to help them. I see people who feel they are treated as second-class citizens because they are poor.

I believe Jesus preached inclusion. This clashes with many conservative evangelicals or those who take the traditional Catholic position, and while I love and respect these people, I admit sometimes I feel ashamed of my Church (in the wider sense). There are huge chasms in our state church on LGBTQ+ issues, which some still consider deeply sinful. I think this is abhorrent, and that telling someone they have a place in hell for being gay is the antithesis of the gospel. There are many people within the Church who would challenge me on this. They will say this is the wrong message. Perhaps I am wrong in wholly supporting gay clergy and same-sex marriage, in supporting those who love someone of the same gender. Perhaps I am wrong in thinking that female clergy should be equal. But I'm prepared to take that risk when it comes to facing my Creator. I don't believe Jesus would condemn anyone for loving, whomever it is they love. I would rather be accused of being too kind in my ministry than too strict. There are parts of scripture that condemn homosexuality; for example, Leviticus Chapter 18, Verse 22 where it states: 'You shall not lie with a male as with a woman; it is an abomination.' When you consider that in other parts of the Bible it says '... children shall be smashed against rocks', well, you learn not to take scripture verbatim, but more as a useful instruction manual and guide to life. The Old Testament was written more than 2,000 years ago. Things were very different back then. In the Bible, we're told not to commit adultery, but many people do, and go on to remarry. There are

Christians who would find that unacceptable. I want my church to be more outward-looking, to engage with the whole community; otherwise the Church of England is in danger of remaining the bastion of white, middle- and upper-class England, i.e. irrelevant to those in my parish and beyond, and particularly those at the bottom of the heap culturally, socially and financially.

When I began going to church, it was in a small village where the congregation was a kind, friendly and safe 'Songs of Praise' crowd, full at Christmas and three-quarters empty for the rest of the year. I passionately wanted to change this, and even the best theologians cannot show me where Jesus preaches in favour of marginalisation. Jesus wanted to bring good news to the poor and suffering, whomever they were.

When I was in the final year of my curacy, at St Matthew's, I was introduced to a non-stipendiary priest, Mother Enid. I asked why she never celebrated Holy Communion, and was told that it wasn't an argument the incumbent Father Mark wanted to have with the congregation. I have every respect for Father Mark, my training incumbent. I think the world of him and understand his reticence. However, that wasn't something I felt I could live with if I was to be appointed the vicar anywhere. And I was perhaps as surprised as anybody when that became a reality at St Matthew's after Father Mark moved on and I was offered the position of vicar in 2018, in the very church I had trained with.

Within a week of taking on my post as vicar, I called a meeting of the Parish Church Council and gave the go-ahead for Mother Enid to celebrate Holy Communion, which was a deeply divisive action and caused much upset. A month later,

Mother Enid became the first female priest ever to celebrate Holy Communion at St Matthew's during a morning mass in autumn 2018. It happened quietly, with little fuss, but it meant an awful lot to her and to me. I don't differentiate between male or female priests, but some members of the church had told me they would leave if we went ahead, which they did.

With any difficult decision, I ask, what would Jesus do? I don't care how much theology people know, no one could ever convince me that Jesus' message was one of marginalisation and exclusion, and so when I was asked to be the training incumbent for Kat, a female priest in a civil partnership, I didn't hesitate. Many in the Church disagree with homosexuality as well as women being ordained. I demur. When I look at Reverend Kat, or Mother Enid, I am unconcerned with gender or sexuality, but focus instead on how we perform as clerics – that's it. That's all that matters.

I wonder sometimes if the Church of England is, in fact, dying a slow death, suffocating itself through its own arrogance and academia. I came to Christianity at the age of 40, with one foot in the 'real' world, and because of this I feel everybody deserves to have a voice, whether they're poor, marginalised, black, queer, gay, whatever. We're all humans. We're all created in God's image, and this is a huge sticking point with our state church. If we believe that everybody is loved in the eyes of God, then there are no pecking orders, no exclusion or judgement. If we, as a church, cannot become inclusive rather than exclusive, then we may well be suffering from a terminal illness. Church attendance is the lowest it has ever been: only around 1 per cent of the UK attends our state church regularly. This is a church of difference and, at times, immorality. We've all heard of priests abusing children or vulnerable members of their congregation; a quick look on Google confirms these things have happened and been covered up. It has taken a pandemic for the Church to make positive changes, to take its message online, to engage with social media, to reach people outside of the church buildings. The Church of England needs to reclaim the positive things it does, for example the many foodbanks it runs, the schools it works with, the lives that are affected in good ways by its teachings, the charities abroad it supports and the overnight shelters. I want people to know about all the wonderful things the Church does, yet the truth is that there is also homophobia, misogyny and racism: these facts are inescapable. I believe the Bible is a wonderful guide for life, and is a great theological book that addresses morality and injustice. I don't, however, believe that everything written there is literally true, but I do believe the gospel of Jesus, in which he tells us to love our neighbour as ourself with all our heart, all our mind, all our soul. He tells us there is no commandment greater than this.

I hope to offer optimism in my ministry because I believe in miracles. That, after all, is the business we are in as Christians, the absolute acceptance that transformation can happen, that we can love each other as equals, that we can all undergo radical change.

I have to believe that those miracles are available to the people I serve. I offer the idea that we can all change and evolve – including the Church itself. I believe we have to role-model Jesus. We have to do what he would do – help those suffering and love everyone regardless of age, race, gender, sexuality or creed. I offer prayers and I appreciate that if you have been brought up to feel worthless, if you're constantly hurt, rejected, unheard and damaged, and you still survive and choose to live, then you can teach us all something about having balls of steel and an iron will, just like Jenny. Yet there is no pill on earth that can restore self-esteem when it has been broken and smashed to the ground throughout your whole life.

Just as I believe people can transform, I feel strongly that we need a complete transformation of the Church, respecting its values and traditions but making change possible. It must become inclusive or risk disappearing altogether. I know my views are deeply controversial. I have received phone calls from people telling me I'll go to hell for my liberal views on same-sex union, and I wonder what Jesus would've made of it. I don't think he would've agreed with my critics; in fact, I think he would have been the first to open his arms to those who love with passion and grace, regardless of their sexuality, gender or colour. These phone calls don't deter me; in fact, they galvanise me. I believe God brought calm to a world created in chaos, though perhaps not to Christmas Eve in a busy high street. I feel the Christian faith gives us the answers to our problems, if we, as a society, choose to hear them. The teachings of Jesus aren't something to put away in a museum; they are living, breathing words and actions.

'So, Father Alex, do ye need a hand at the church? When my youngest goes to school or what-not, I'd like to come and volunteer,' Jenny said, biting into her biscuit.

For a moment I was stunned.

'That'd be amazing, Jenny,' I spluttered. 'Though how on earth will ye find the time?'

'Oh don't worry, I'll be rait,' Jenny replied.

I looked over at Judy, who has 10 kids yet somehow finds the time to help out on the estate each holiday, helping to run the Fit and Fed Club, buttering butties and pouring drinks for the local children who might otherwise not have a lunchtime meal. To say I was humbled just sounds crass, but I was. Jesus' message of love was loud and clear in the living, breathing actions of these women and so many others like them across the country.

6.

BROKEN

'Come to me, all you who are weary and
burdened, and I will give you rest.'

Matthew 11:28

Knocking on Rosemary and Ian's door, I couldn't help but
notice the state of the small house they were living in. It was
a normal red-brick terraced property but there were weeds
growing everywhere and a fridge freezer was sitting in the
small front yard. It seemed obvious the family was still struggling. They only lived a few streets away, so I had decided to
walk though it was freezing cold with dull skies and relent-
less drizzle. I walked along the rows of houses, dodging the
kids on oversized electric scooters and every now and then
being growled at by an angry bull terrier of some description.
I was grateful for the garden gates as the only things sitting
between me and the animals with teeth sharper than the
knife bin I passed just moments earlier. I quickened my pace,
passing rubbish bins overflowing with empty bottles and
food containers. In the grey light of the day, the streets with

straggling weeds and bits of stray rubbish looked bleaker than ever.

Rosemary opened the door and ushered me inside, immediately offering to make coffee for us.

'What's to do? Are ye alright?' I said, as I walked down the dark, cramped hallway into the dining area next to a tiny galley kitchen. There was a washing machine churning away at the back of the 'two-up, two-down' and a huge pile of washing sitting beside it. In that moment, I got a sense of the enormity of everyday survival, not just for Rosemary who was no doubt doing all that washing, but for them all. There was little decoration in the room except for a table and chairs, a dog bed, and toys that seemed to be spilling out of the corner. Two of the younger children were playing on the floor, so I smiled at them as they carried on with their game. An enormous dog barked in the front room, and I was glad that the door was shut.

'Have a seat, Father. It's nice of ye to drop by,' Rosemary said, again giving me that sad smile.

'It's good to be here. Thanks for inviting me in,' I said. 'How's things for ye all? I wanted to check in and say hello, see how you're all doin'.'

'Oh, we're alright,' Rosemary started to say, but then the sound of barking got instantly noisier, and I realised the lounge door was being opened, then quickly shut. Ian appeared, and though he was skinny he seemed to fill the doorway.

'Oh hello, Ian. I didn't realise you were home,' I said, smiling. Ian nodded but didn't reply. It was half eleven on a Monday morning, and I wondered whether he was working at the minute or not. I didn't know what it was, but there seemed to be an air of brooding anger about this man. I knew from other conversations I'd managed to have with Rosemary that he had anger-management problems, as she put it. He seemed to be a very unhappy man, and I started to see how that might affect the whole household, especially as they were forced to share such a small space together.

Just then the older twins Layton and Lucy appeared. They nodded in my direction then asked their mother for some food.

'I'll make ye both a butty. Here, Ian, come and sit with Father Alex, will ye,' Rosemary said before stepping into the kitchen and opening a loaf of cheap white bread. Ian looked like it was the last thing he wanted to do, but to give him credit he came and sat with me. In some ways, I was pleased to have this chance to speak with him. I didn't know if I could help this family, but I wanted to try, even if just to listen.

'Alright, Father. Have ye seen any good films recently?' Ian said. I looked at him incredulously.

'Er no, I don't think I have. I haven't been to the pictures in ages. Have you seen any?' I stuttered. I had come to see this family in the hope of talking about their problems, and how we might work together to encourage Lucy to attend school, yet not only did it appear that Lucy wasn't there, neither was her twin brother, and their dad was trying to talk to me about films! It doesn't happen often, but at that moment I wanted to shake him. I wanted to ask him why he would think about films when he had bigger problems to contend with.

'So, I see the twins aren't at school today. Are they ill?' I said as kindly as I could.

Ian shrugged.

'They've got behavioural issues so they don't go to school no more,' he said.

'Yes, I can see. Can anyone at the school help you?' I asked, sipping the coffee Rosemary had made me.

'They've tried but there's nowt they can do. They don't want to go ...'

The twins were standing in the kitchen eating the butties their mum had made them, and I was conscious they could hear every word.

'He's got no work at the minute so we're skint as well, Father,' Rosemary said from the doorway leading to the galley. 'We've no money.'

'I'm sorry to hear that, Rosemary,' I said quietly. 'Listen, if there's any way I can help, by ringing the school or council, please let me know.' I couldn't think of anything else to say.

The visit went quickly after that. I felt utterly dispirited and helpless in the face of Ian's apathy, and the way he seemed to be so unconcerned about his children's education and, ultimately, their future. He looked like a drifter, happy to watch the world go by with no ambition to make his life, or his kids' lives, better. Then again, I had no idea what demons he was struggling with. I said goodbye and walked back to the church, through the streets. People said 'Hello Father' as they do, and I smiled and said hello to a few, but my mind was whirling with what I'd witnessed. Their lives appeared to me to be broken, and I didn't have a clue how to help them fix things without some input from them, without some encouragement or drive. I could see Rosemary loved her children, and wanted the best for them, but Ian was different. Somehow, I felt that he expected the world to contribute to him rather than the other way around. I'd invited the two eldest to our church study group for youngsters in the hope that might inspire them and help them feel safe in a group setting again, and I fervently hoped they'd come as I left that day.

As parents we are products of our own upbringings. I noticed that Rosemary and Ian talked openly about their struggles in front of the children. There seemed to be no boundaries, no sense that the children's issues should not be talked about in front of them either. When we had bumped into each other in the local park on another occasion, they had openly discussed the fact the teenagers don't attend school and have behavioural issues, despite the twins standing beside them. Part of me worries that this becomes a self-fulfilling prophecy, and does nothing to inspire their children into attending school. I came away from that brief chat with real concerns about Ian. He's always very polite to me, but if you could see the family you'd get a sense of how things really are behind closed doors.

I know a lot of people in my parish who could work but don't. It has become normalised to live on benefits and not work. I always joke that I'm a right-wing socialist because I want people to rise above their circumstances and create better lives for themselves and their families, yet we have to find meaningful ways of supporting them to do this. We don't, as a society, address the root cause as to why people don't work. There are loads of vacancies in Burnley, lots of jobs up for grabs, yet people simply aren't taking them. I understand that the poverty trap created by benefits that penalise attempts to work is a big factor, but there are other factors. With my Argos Manager hat on, and thinking about Root Cause Analysis, I might suggest that people are not equipped to work. There are many who are not emotionally or mentally mature enough to take on positions. They have perhaps been broken by their lives, by family breakdowns, by poverty and scarcity, by trauma or inadequate schooling. They're not physically prepared to be out there making their own way. There is a kind of malaise, a melancholy or lethargy, that I see in some of the people who come to my church, like Ian and his family. If your life has been chaotic or troubled, or hopeless or impoverished, these conditions of life do not prepare you to enter the workplace and make something of yourself. If this has been the way things are through your teenage years, then you're hardly going to be inclined to get up and do a 38.5-hour week for minimum wage, are you? If the option is to do nothing and be given the bare minimum to survive on, then people will do that if they haven't been exposed or equipped to do anything else. If we aim at nothing, then we'll surely gain it. Why bother even raising the bow and arrow? What I used to love about my job at Argos was seeing the Christmas temps come in. Many had limited skill sets at the beginning, but with training and perseverance some went on to have managerial roles in the company and wonderful careers. How incredible is that? It shows that with the right support people can achieve beyond what is expected of them.

'Is that Father Alex?' said the young female voice on the telephone not long after I'd got back from seeing the troubled family.

'It is. How can I help?' I replied.

'It's Milena. Can I please come and see you?' she asked.

'Of course you can,' I replied, happy to see this young lady at church again. Milena and her partner Ivan were planning their wedding at St Matthew's for the summer and were regular church attendees, which had thrilled our congregation, who are always glad to see new blood in the church.

When the woman arrived, I saw instantly that something was wrong.

'Sit down and have a brew,' I said, bustling around the kitchen, trying to find the tea bags.

'I'm sorry to come but I have to speak to someone ...'

'That's okay, that's my job. You're always welcome, you know that,' I said, smiling, and wondering what could be bothering this woman. On the outside the couple had everything. They'd bought their terraced house, which was only a few streets away, and spent their spare hours and money in doing it up. It was a lovely home and now they were planning on building a life together. Ivan was a very charming, polite man, and they seemed perfect together. It goes to show how deceptive appearances can be.

'It's Ivan. When I met him, I knew about his problem with gambling. He'd said it was all in the past, but he's been found stealing from work. He's been taking timber from the warehouse and selling it online. The company found out and it's all come out. He has also been borrowing money from his family, tens of thousands of pounds, to fund his secret gambling, and now that's all come out too. He owes money to a loan shark and we can't pay it. What should I do?'

At this, Milena, a slim woman in her twenties with long blonde hair, broke down. Sobbing now, she could barely speak. I admit I was stunned. Most addictions to substances, like drugs and alcohol, just can't be hidden, not in the damaging later stages at least. It struck me that I would never have guessed there was anything amiss with this man who'd I'd met several times as the couple had become regular churchgoers. It was obvious he'd even managed to hide it all from his bride-to-be, and the revelation that he was in big trouble was ground-shaking. I took a deep breath and waited before replying to her question, knowing I would be giving her an answer she probably wouldn't want to hear.

'If there are issues in a relationship around trust or integrity, then you should call the marriage off. At least, postpone it for the time being while all this is happening, but gambling is an addiction and it is hard to overcome.'

Milena nodded though she was still crying. We sat there for a while, until the young woman felt ready to go back and face the world.

'Ye can always come and speak to me. I'll speak to Ivan too, if that would help?'

Again, she nodded, though we both knew that her life was about to change radically. The couple never appeared again at church, and the wedding was cancelled. To this day, none of our congregation knows what happened to them.

It's devastating when a wedding is called off, except in the case when I was asked by the couple to have an eagle at the ceremony.

'An eagle! What do you want that for?' I said, incredulously.

'Well, me friend runs a bird of prey centre and might be able to get us an eagle to perch in the church, then fly down with the rings and land on your arm,' said the groom-to-be with a perfectly straight face.

I laughed, thinking it was a joke. It wasn't.

'We want the eagle to land on your arm while you're performing the ceremony,' the bride-to-be added, helpfully.

I looked at them both. They were a young couple and we're always wanting younger people to join the church so I agreed to look it up.

'Okay, though I'm not really sure how I feel about a massive great big eagle landing on my arm while I'm in my vestments,' I added. I was convinced there would be a get-out clause, 'Thou shalt have no eagles in church', or something like that, but there was nothing. It was perfectly legal and allowed. My heart sank. When they rang a few days later to cancel the wedding, I'd be lying if I said I wasn't delighted.

Burnley is a place of extremes. We have some of the highest levels of deprivation in Lancashire and also some affluent areas. Victoria and Richard show that appearances aren't always right, and that people and lives are broken everywhere, in so many ways.

For many of my parishioners, it tends to be rock bottom that hits when tragedy or problems strike. People are falling through the gaps here, and no one seems to care.

Mark reappeared one Saturday morning.

'Alright,' he said, coming up to me, limping heavily.

'Mark, I've been worried about ye. You weren't in any of your usual places,' I said. I'd been out in my car looking for him because I hadn't seen him for a while.

'Oh I've got new accommodation but it's no good. They nick my benefits and buy crack with it. Everyone there is at it,' he replied. He looked terrible. His face appeared battered, he had a massive black eye and he was physically shaking. The whole of the left side of his face was black and blue. His nose was still bloody and he looked like he'd had a proper kicking. Apparently, he'd moved into some grim accommodation, some chalets in a pretty desperate neighbourhood where there were always lots of fights. I've taken a funeral for someone from those chalets who'd ended their own life in one of the flats; someone who overdosed and died on a park bench. It was a notorious area where Mark was surrounded by similar people and where drugs were rife; in fact he had a count-up one day and informed me that 18 of the 25 residents were, in his words, 'crackheads'.

'There was a fight last night, and I got this,' he said, pointing shakily at his face.

'I can see that, Mark; you look a state. I've got some nutrition drinks given to me by a member of my congregation whose relative passed away. Let me grab you a few. I bet ye can't remember when ye last ate.' Mark took the drinks.

'I don't want to live like this any more,' he said, eventually. 'I can't live like this, I'm goin' to die.'

'Well, that's something, Mark. I'm so glad to hear ye say that. You can't go on like this. You're going to die if you carry on and I don't want to be here taking your funeral,' I replied.

He revealed to me that his problems probably started in childhood when as a small boy he saw many awful things: drugs, crime and violence. What child could witness that and be unaffected? Where was the support for him he so badly needed at a young age? Mark is yet another individual who has been failed by the system, and left to flounder in his trauma and addictions. I know things are never as simple as that, but I cannot help feeling, the longer I know him, that he could've had a useful, happy life if only there had been someone who'd cared enough for his wellbeing.

By the end of our chat he was in a marginally better state than he'd arrived in, but what did give me hope was that he was finally saying he didn't want to live like that any longer.

He asked for my help, help I was willing to give, but what could I actually do?

The first thing I did was get on the phone. I called several agencies, most of whom knew of Mark. Shockingly, the response I had was at best apathetic. One of the people I spoke to even said he was a lost cause and was just going to die. That wasn't good enough for me, it wasn't something I was just going to accept. The services might have failed Mark and those like him, but I was determined that the Church wouldn't. I had an idea that if we showed someone what life could be like, there might be an epiphany moment for the individual. I got back on the phone and began to ring round local treatment centres; that was entirely against all protocol, but I had to do something or watch my broken friend die before my eyes.

Perhaps we, as a society, are weary and burdened, and are needing rest and respite. I know that Mark is weary and burdened, worn out by his life, by surviving. I know Rosemary and Judy are weary. Both lovely women who look exhausted at times. I know Jenny is burdened, and how could she not be? This is where our state church should be; creating a place of refuge that acts as a beacon of light to communities across the country. It is my view that we need to place spirituality and the sacred at the heart of decision-making, and in that way we start to build a better society, a fairer society.

7.

CALLING

'He leads me beside quiet waters,
he refreshes my soul.
He guides me along the right paths
for his name's sake.'

Psalm 23, 1–3

The conversation that started my journey as a Christian happened after taking my daughter to Sunday school twelve years ago. I admit I went reluctantly, but when I stepped inside the church I felt a sense of peace. Life was really hectic then. I had three young children and a busy job with Argos while I was also moonlighting as a second-division stand-up comic in bars and dodgy venues across the North. I sat in the service as my daughter went to her class and the sermon was about 'loving thy neighbour'. It was Jesus' gospel, his message of good news, and something about it struck me. It was so different to every other aspect of my life. Weirdly, I enjoyed the service, and at the end the vicar came over to me.

'You're a new face,' he said. I later discovered he was called Reverend Richard.

'Well, yes, sort of,' I stuttered, not at all sure I wanted to speak to a vicar.

'Why don't you come to the vicarage for a coffee?' He smiled, as if he could read my thoughts.

'Noooooo,' I screamed in my mind.

'Yes, that would be lovely,' I said.

Something strange happened on the way home. As I drove, I was mulling the service over when I spotted suspicious activity in my neighbour's garden and so, the sermon's message still playing in my mind, I called the police. It turned out that in fact there was a robbery taking place. I know that if I hadn't heard that sermon I may never have thought to help my neighbour.

That first chat with a priest was excruciating. I'd never been inside a vicarage before, but I know now that you can't walk into a vicarage without being slapped in the face by a picture of the blessed Virgin Mary or a representation of Jesus on the cross, and this place was no different. He sat me in his office while he went to make a brew. The study was filled with books and with crosses, which I eyed nervously. I remember hearing the boiling kettle, the stirring of a spoon, and it was like time stood still. It was like waiting for a really important interview to commence, one that I knew I was going to fail.

What am I doing in this room? I thought. Do I have to repent of all my sins, because that could take a while. The only things I knew about vicars were from the telly. Reverend Richard did none of that. We chatted for a while. I told him about my three kids and that I was working for Argos. He asked me why I'd gone to church. I told him that in the short space of time I'd been coming to his services I enjoyed it. I felt better afterwards than I did before, and so I kept coming. At this point there was nothing spiritual going on. He asked me what I knew about the Bible, and I replied that I knew nothing at all except I once played the role of Caspar – one of the Three Kings – in the school Nativity play. We talked about comedy and that's when he asked me if I watched *The Vicar of Dibley*, and did I know the theme tune, to which I replied, 'Yes.'

That's when he told me the theme music was the 23rd Psalm, 'The Lord is my shepherd'.

The Lord is my shepherd, I lack nothing.
He makes me lie down in green pastures, he leads me
beside quiet waters, he refreshes my soul.
He guides me along the right paths for his name's sake.

At that first meeting I didn't know one psalm from another, but this verse has come to mean a lot to me, though it meant nothing back then.

'Do you know the psalm?' Reverend Richard smiled, stirring his tea.

'I don't, I'm afraid,' I replied. 'I don't know anything about the Church, except for churchy words like gospel, Matthew, Mark, Luke and John. The only thing I know about Genesis is that Phil Collins was a drummer of good standing, and the Girgashites sound like a bowel condition ...'

There was a brief moment of silence as the reverend digested my words. I blushed, sure I had offended him.

'Ah, I see,' he said simply and sipped his drink, his eyes

twinkling. For a moment, I was convinced he was going to shout at me because I didn't know anything.

'It's a lovely psalm. Why don't you go away and read it, then make some notes and come back? We can talk more about it then.'

Again, every part of me screamed 'no', but I found myself nodding.

'Do you need to borrow a Bible?' he said, that smile still on his face.

'Er, yes I do, Father, thank you,' I replied as I took the offered tome and scuttled out of his office.

I didn't read it straight away, but when I finally did I found myself thinking of the line from 'Gangsta's Paradise' by Coolio: 'As I walk through the valley of the shadow of death, I take a look at my life, and realise there's nothin' left ...' Until that moment, I thought Coolio had written it. As I preferred to listen to audible books because of my dyslexia, I went out to the local charity shops and brought up all the Aled Jones CDs. If you're ever short of an Aled Jones CD, then get yourself down to a charity shop, because they're full of them. Katherine Jenkins was there too. I found her CD in the local British Heart Foundation. I began playing the psalm in the car. I love poetry but I've never read any religious poetry, except for the lyrics by Depeche Mode's Martin Gore, who writes songs of religious ambiguity that always intrigued me.

I went back to see Reverend Richard a couple of weeks later, and he explained to me how important the psalm is to millions of Christians. It is a psalm sung or read at weddings and funerals, and I now use it a lot as well in my services. The words offer hope and suggestion beyond what we are here for in the here and now. We need hope. We need a Christian metaphor for light in the darkness. I feel that hope can't be found in our politicians at the moment. I feel it is the Church that must lead the way, offering optimism and faith where there is turmoil and conflict. The darkness has yet to win. Throughout history, the light has always won, has always shone brightest. I have a very simple way of reminding myself of this. I keep the sanctuary candle burning in church all year. It is always lit, so in the dark of the winter months, whenever I feel hopeless, depressed or defeated, I just have to go into the church and see that candle. The Church is not here to offer just immediate hope, or hope for the future; we are in the business of eternal hope, of eternal life. We believe that after we've lived life we enter the house of the Lord. I like that thought. And it isn't just hope for a 'believer', it is hope for everyone, whether they believe or not.

That coffee with Reverend Richard was the start of everything. That psalm was the beginning for me. God was shepherding me into becoming a priest, into leading and caring for my sometimes bizarre, sometimes downright offensive and humorous flock. That conversation changed my life. When we do go astray, when we've wandered off life's perfect path, he's there telling us, there's always a way back. I find that incredibly comforting. By 2010, I had been baptised by Reverend Richard. Afterwards he gave a sermon alluding to the fact that true disciples of Jesus have to give their life to him. I remember thinking, I can't do that, he's having a laugh. I can give him an occasional Sunday but apart from that ...' Despite my initial reaction, I quickly decided I wanted to be confirmed. This is a special service in which the promises made at baptism, to commit to a life following Jesus, are remade. When I was confirmed, the presiding bishop gave a beautiful sermon about the Road to Damascus story. It is the story of conversion. I don't like the word 'conversion' because it reminds me of 'Conversion Therapy', which I am fundamentally opposed to, but I really love the tale, which says we can all change. We can all evolve. The story goes that Saul, a Pharisee who until then had tormented the followers of Jesus and wanted to wipe them out, was travelling in search of more Christians to persecute and was met by Jesus on the road between Damascus and Jerusalem. Saul was blinded by the light of Jesus and was sent away. A few days later his sight was restored and the scales fell away from them. He would go on to be one of Jesus' supreme devotees. Paul experienced a miracle, an act of revelation, a complete conversion to Christianity even though he was en route to arrest followers of Jesus in Damascus. He is now viewed as one of the greatest disciples, and his story is a huge inspiration to me. I never did have a blinding 'Road to Damascus' experience, but the calling came nonetheless.

Becoming a vicar was never something I'd ever thought I would aim for. That's how I know it was an authentic calling. I tried to ignore it because I was convinced it was beyond the realms of possibility for me with my lack of formal education. My stand-up show was actually doing quite well, and I'd attracted an agent who made a few bookings for me. My faith was creeping in, though, and after a couple of gigs, one where I'd been overshadowed by the late arrival of a 99 ice cream van, and another where the heckler got a bigger laugh than I did, I realised that my calling was growing stronger, and my ambitions with comedy and with Argos were falling away.

Reverend Richard and I had become good friends. We were out walking our dogs together along the river one fine autumnal day when I asked him, 'So, what's it like being a vicar?'

'I wondered when you were going to ask!'

I came away from that conversation thinking it all sounded very nice but far beyond me and my capabilities. You usually have to get a degree, which felt like a joke in itself. I left school at the age of 15 with no qualifications, nothing. I was so bad at maths they had to create a new bottom set for me. How could I possibly become a priest?

'So, Sarah, have ye got a moment?' I asked my wife not long after that riverside chat with Reverend Richard.

'Yes, Alex, what is it?' Sarah said. We were settling down in front of the telly after the kids were all in bed and it seemed like the perfect opportunity.

'Um, I'm thinking of becoming a vicar ...' Best to come straight out with it.

'A vicar? Are ye really, Alex?' she replied carefully. I had to give her credit. I had a well-paid, full-time job that afforded us a nice home and holidays, yet I was basically saying I wanted to jack it all in and do something that looked to be almost impossible for me.

'Yes, I think I want to train as a priest,' I said, barely able to meet her eyes. Even I thought I sounded like I was having some sort of breakdown. 'Actually, I think I'm being called to be a priest.'

There was a pause. When Sarah eventually replied, her voice was steady though she must've been pretty dumbfounded. Since meeting her I'd wanted to be a ref, a comedian and now a rev.

'Why don't ye give it some more thought? You've not been going to church very long,' she said, eventually.

I did give it more thought, and over the weeks the calling felt stronger, so I began my journey with more than a little trepidation. I knew I wasn't clever enough to become a vicar, which the Church initially affirmed. Reverend Richard encouraged me to enrol on a low-level church course, which would give me a certificate. To someone like me with no exam success whatsoever, there is nothing more glorious than a certificate. As part of this course I had to write essays. Oh my God, they were terrible! I struggled, so much so I was only one phone call away from jacking it all in. This wasn't anywhere like degree level, it was Saturday-afternoon, sub-GCSE level and I still couldn't do it. So, I sent an email saying I was leaving the course but the tutor rang me and told me she didn't want me to stop. She told me I just had to keep going and she would help me. It took me many more months of endeavour and I finally made it. God knows how but I did, I scraped through, and I got that certificate.

I then met with the Director of Ordinands, who oversees those who come forward for ministerial training. It was at that point that I thought, maybe I can actually do this. It was eventually agreed that I could go forward to the Bishop's Advisory Panel, which is basically a 48-hour interrogation by various people from the Church – the bishop, priests and lay people – to discern if I had actually been called to study for the priesthood. I was intensely nervous, though both my wife and Reverend Richard were supporting me. Nothing can prepare you for the discussion panel. You have to walk out with the panel's blessing or you cannot move any further forward.

Arriving at Shallowford retreat house in Staffordshire, I realised I was surrounded by middle-class England: Earl Grey and Rooibos tea bags, and the Marks & Spencer's Springwear collection. The experience was unnerving and overwhelming.

I was straight back into being that boy who walked into the exam hall to find there was no table set out for me. I'm doomed, is all I could think. My future was in the hands of these people and if it all went terribly wrong, which I already suspected it would, then I'd have to wait another three to four years to try again.

'Hello, I'm Alex Frost,' I said, nervously, to the group of wannabe-priests. It was like being on *Big Brother*. I could feel myself being watched.

'Hello, I'm Alex Frost,' I said to the bishops who were overseeing the weekend.

'Now, you've been picked to speak last this afternoon. It might be worth spending some time preparing ...' one of the clergymen said to me. I scurried off, spent a couple of hours getting more nervous, then joined the group.

'... and that's why flowers are so important to ministry and in honouring an individual's humanity and experience ...'

The guy before me had spoken beautifully about flowers! Everyone clapped heartily. It was finally my turn.

'I'm going to talk to you about the repression of homosexuality in Uganda ...' I began. I gabbled my way through my presentation, hardly daring to look up from my notes.

'And this is why we must become a church of inclusion and embrace the political and global stage ...' I finished, cringing.

There was absolute silence. In short, my presentation was a complete car crash.

No one spoke. No one clapped.

'And how do you engage with these matters at your local church?' asked the bishop. All eyes swivelled to me.

'Erm, well we don't really ... we have a great kids' club though,' I stammered.

'Well, okay, tell us about that,' the bishop said, eyebrows raised almost to his hairline.

'Erm, well, it's called the KKK Club ...' Before I could continue, the bishop cleared his throat.

'The KKK Club? Are you sure it's called that?'

'Yes, of course,' I blustered and carried on, my head spinning, while inside I was dying a slow, painful death, worse than even my most dire performance as a stand-up, where at the Frog and Bucket Club in Manchester I limped to the stage in character as a traffic warden and got heckled off before I'd said a single gag. My mind had gone blank. When it was over I went back to my room and realised what I'd said. The group was called the Triple H Club, and I'd said it was named after the racist, terrorist, white supremacy group, the Ku Klux Klan. What a massive idiot.

It came as no surprise when I was rejected. The one small chink of hope was that they asked me to return in 12 months – which at the time felt like no consolation at all – and it was suggested that I enrol on a course of academic study at degree level in the meantime. When I enrolled as an independent student, I discovered I would be with the same people who had been selected, including the chap who had spoken so nicely about flowers. I was sent on placement to St Matthew's to learn about the traditions, a place I could never have believed I would one day be vicar of. I went back in front of that panel a year later to be told I'd done well enough academically on the course. But another fail. I was told to go away and study for a further year.

By this time I was thoroughly pissed off. I thought about jacking it all in, but I couldn't. I was determined to get there one day, so I continued studying for another year. If there's one word that sums up my path to becoming a priest, it's 'failure'. I've always said I was designed for middle management. I've never been brilliant, and I've never been completely shit. I've rarely won an award, I'm basically mediocre, which is rather troublesome as it makes the highs and lows of life somewhat of a challenge. At some point in my life, I decided in my own mind it was probably best to be mediocre, occasionally putting my head above the parapet, but mostly keeping it down and plodding on with life. There's so much joy in being kind, in being gentle, and I've finally found a place where those qualities are valued, though it took me until second or third time round to get there. In many ways, I wouldn't change my journey, looking back, though it was incredibly hard at the time. It proved to me how much I wanted the priesthood. Even so, I think it says something about how we at the Church of England treat people who are different from the usual, white, middle-class mould. I feel that overlooking people who aren't academic means that those of us who have more practical and pastoral skills are ignored. I resent that, as I know many people who would make wonderful priests but who would never know how to put an apostrophe in the right place or words in the right order. Should this be the criteria for selecting a vicar? I don't think it should. So, again, I studied as an independent student, which meant I had to pay for my own study, and watched my peer group move ever closer to ordination. I was made to drive to Gateshead, where in the shadow of the Angel of the North I met with the Bishop of Jarrow. I nearly didn't go as I assumed I'd be rejected again, but he really seemed to understand me. He was lovely, and it was he who invited me to train for the priesthood and start the formative training period of three years that would lead to my eventual ordination.

With three young children by now, I realised I couldn't hope to live on a church grant so I continued to work full time at Argos while studying for my Theology Degree. It was tough. Every week I'd have to drive to Lancaster, and every eight weeks I had to go to a residential course at Rydal Hall at Ambleside in the Lake District. Those dates naturally always seemed to fall on birthdays or anniversaries, and it was hard for everyone around me. Again, I struggled with the essay-writing. I scraped pass marks, just over the 40 mark, and was surrounded by people complaining that they'd done badly because they only got a 60. I continued to feel like a failure, and, despite the pain, I'm grateful for that feeling. I know what it is to be what society would consider a failure. I know how it feels, how sharp that particular pain can be. My journey makes sense to me now, and it's why I feel I've been called to serve the people I do every day in my parish: the poor, the disenfranchised, the fractured and broken, the unvalued. I felt unvalued. I felt disenfranchised from the middle-class Earl-Grey-tea culture of the Church of England even while God guided me to the priesthood. I felt ignored and rejected. To be a good priest we have to be able to understand, we have to be able to be kind, to empathise with the difficulties in life that our parishioners experience on a daily basis. My parishioners don't survive month to month. It's not even week to week for some, it's day to day, hour to hour. It's a battle, and in some ways I understand how very unfair that battle against everything can feel, how difficult it is to be constantly judged as inadequate or inferior, because I've felt all those things too.

When Rosemary and Ian turned up with their eldest, twins Layton and Lucy, at my church study group, I was thrilled, but it soon became clear that they would struggle even with our little group.

'So, what's your favourite telly programme?' I asked to get the kids chatting and help them feel comfortable.

All the hands went up except Layton and Lucy's.

I asked a few of the children, who spoke passionately and excitedly about various programmes on CBBC, then turned to the twins.

'Lucy, what's your favourite programme?' She shrugged, and my heart sank.

'I dunno,' was all she said.

'Layton, perhaps you know? Do you know Lucy's favourite show, or do you have one to share?' If anything, Layton looked more uncomfortable than his sister. He shrugged, and I felt like I'd lost the battle or the war, or something.

I tried to gee them up but it was clear they struggled with the social interaction, and my heart bled for them. Perhaps, in time, they'll grow to enjoy it or get something from it, or perhaps not. I was trying to lead them to quiet waters, to something that might unlock their potential, that might, as the verse says, refresh their soul. I could guide them but I could not do the work for them.

8.

THY WILL BE DONE

'your kingdom come,
your will be done,
on earth as it is in heaven.'

Matthew 6:10

'How dare ye shut the fuckin' church! How dare ye leave us out here, without the church! It's a fuckin' disgrace. You're a vicar, ye can open those doors right now!'

I didn't recognise the woman who was screaming at me. She appeared just after I'd popped out to get provisions from a local shop, wearing my dog collar because I'd just led a service on Zoom, and the clergy had been made designated key workers. The first lockdown had hit us all hard. There was profound disbelief at the enforced isolation and regulations needed to keep people safe.

'I'm really sorry. The bishop has told us we must close. Public safety is our main concern; I'm so sorry you feel this way,' I said, clutching my bag of loo roll and bananas.

If anything, this statement riled her more. The woman was becoming increasingly agitated by the second, gesticulating and swearing loudly.

'Ye shouldn't fuckin' shut the church. Ye don't give a shit about us, do ye? None of ye give a fuckin' shit what happens to us out here.' I'd started to walk a bit faster. The woman was probably ten years younger than me, dressed in leggings and a hoodie, but she was furious; not just angry, but furious.

In my heart, I wasn't at all sure I didn't agree with her. The order to close the doors of St Matthew's had troubled me deeply. I imagine it was the first time in the church's history that its congregation, or someone like this woman who wasn't a regular but who that day obviously needed to access the church, was barred from it. Had the Church of England made a terrible mistake? I didn't have time to ponder it. The woman started to grab at my sleeve and I thought she might attack me as she launched into yet another tirade. Sometimes, wearing a dog collar makes priests quite vulnerable. Other people recognise us, they know who we are, but we don't know them. I didn't know what this woman was capable of, or whether she had some kind of mental health condition underlying her strong emotions.

'Look, I'm sorry. It wasn't my decision. If I could've kept St Matthew's open, I would've.'

She spat at the ground, and snarled: 'Just excuses!'

I ran to my car. By the time I got there I was shaking with fear and feeling extremely distressed. The move to shut the churches because of this awful new virus called Covid 19 had left me troubled, wondering if we were abandoning our flock at exactly the time they needed us most. What I'd said to her was true, though. At my ordination, I swore an oath to my bishop to obey him, and that's what I had done. Trembling, I drove back to the vicarage, but I was starting to understand that the impact of the virus would be far greater than I'd imagined.

The lockdown was a rude awakening not long after returning from a pilgrimage to the Holy Land. In Jerusalem, we kept hearing reports of a strange new virus, and I kept thinking it'd blow over. It didn't blow over. It became a tornado that has ripped through our lives, lives already fragile, lives already fragmented and broken, and left a trail of utter devastation. The trip had made real all the things I had studied agonisingly over the years before I was finally ordained. In those heady days before Covid struck us like a hammer blow, I took a photo of myself in a dog collar for the first time to post on Facebook, still unable to believe my ordination was really happening. After all the tears, tantrums, upsets and joys, the culmination of the hours spent reading obscure theological texts and learning to write essays that weren't terrible had finally arrived. It was the best day of my life apart from the birth of my children. All my Argos peers were there, along with my 95-year-old granny and my extended family and childhood friends. A service of Holy Communion was celebrated, and I took the Vows of Ordination, where I knelt in front of the Bishop of Blackburn. The bishop laid his hands on me and ordained me into holy orders. It was incredibly moving. I really felt that I was part of the community of thousands and thousands of people across the world across the centuries who have entered holy orders. The bishop said the words: 'I ordain you in the name of the Father, Son and Holy Spirit.' As the service finished, the cathedral bells rang out. I felt like I'd won the lottery. They call it the time of formation after being ordained, but I already felt formed, I felt ready to serve. Here I was, serving the Church and the community the only way I knew how, but to serve one I was now being asked to fail the other, or that's how it felt that day. Even as I drove away, I could see the woman trying to chase my car, her face screwed up in rage, and I felt I was letting her down despite everything.

Everything became difficult. I queued for an hour to get into Tesco, and there was the one-way system along the aisles. The last time I queued for that long was for the Nemesis ride at Alton Towers. I imagine most of us fell into the trap of panic-buying as the news was filled with fear stories, tales of empty supermarket shelves and empty shops. Then came lockdown, and access to all the things we would consider to be normality – bars, restaurants, the pictures, shopping malls – was stopped. Burnley became like a ghost town. One morning I found myself driving around at 6am looking for loo rolls.

That Easter of 2020, I celebrated the dawn Eucharist from the side of my house and streamed it live on social media. From that moment onwards, we became extremely proactive in taking the church online. My curate, Reverend Kat, and I drew up a spreadsheet of all the people on our register, and rang them weekly to make contact; meanwhile we took our services online. At the time, everything was restricted and we were only allowed out for one hour of freedom daily, and we worried about a lot of our regular churchgoers who lived alone and were already isolated. The new rhythm of life became the new normality.

I met a family who had fallen through society's cracks. I'd received a call from a local headteacher asking me to check in on a European family who couldn't speak much English as she'd been worried about them over lockdown. As soon as the restrictions eased, she asked me to go over there and see how they were. The teacher had various concerns mostly centring around the family's level of poverty, and so I popped round to their rented accommodation. I wonder if slum land-lords will be the next big health and political scandal; if they aren't then they should be. I walked up to their terraced house on a typical street nearby. There were no curtains in the windows. A woman opened the door and I tried to explain who I was. Her English was very limited but, luckily, she let me in, and as I walked through that small home, my mask covering half my face, I was shocked at how they were living. I was trying to smile and make stilted conversation, though my mask kept steaming up as I hadn't yet got the knack of wearing it with my glasses. The young boy translated halt-ingly but we made some progress and they told me what had happened to them. They had nothing. They had less than nothing in fact.

There was no furniture in the house at all; no carpet, no settee, no television, no radio, no books, nothing. There weren't even lampshades, just a bare bulb in each room hang-ing down from the ceiling. The parents and their child had been sharing a single bed as they couldn't afford to buy another. It was nothing short of destitution. Before the lock-down, both parents had been working in the food industry, but they'd been laid off. They didn't know they were entitled to benefits, and were receiving nothing. To get by, they'd borrowed money off family, but they were now literally living off nothing. Shock and horror overwhelmed me.

The phone rang and rang. I was put on hold for what seemed like hours. I was desperately calling every helpline I could find, and was now tackling Social Services on the family's behalf. Finally, someone picked up.

'Hello, it's Father Alex Frost. I need to talk to someone about getting benefits for a family who desperately need them. They don't speak much English, which is why I'm calling. Can you please help? I've been waiting for nearly an hour on the line,' I said, trying to keep my voice steady though inside I was raging. I was raging because of the shock, because of the unfairness, because this family had simply received no support.

I turned back to the family, who were watching me wide-eyed. The mother was a slight woman dressed in traditional clothing, while her husband was in Western clothes, and their son, a sweet lad of probably six or seven, watched quietly while sitting on his mother's lap.

'It's okay, it'll all be okay once we get ye in the system,' I said, though I honestly couldn't imagine how it could be okay.

'Thank you, thank you,' the mother, called Raji, said in broken English, her hands in the praying gesture, held together though nothing else in their lives was.

'Yes, hello? Hello? It's Father Alex Frost. Yes, ye can speak to the family, but what I'm tryin' to tell ye is they don't speak much English ...'

This went on for a while, but finally, after plenty of to-ing and fro-ing, we made progress, and their benefit claim was started. I could not help thinking that without someone like me, a third party, a vicar, who on earth would be helping them? Apparently, nobody. The benefits system seemed almost designed to be complicated, and difficult to navigate, and they wouldn't have had a chance doing it by themselves.

The worst thing was, I knew they must be one family of so many across my parish and across the country that were falling through the seismic cracks in our system. I know from experience there are many families in certain parts of the United Kingdom where English is not the first language. At my own church school, we are a diverse community with lots of different nationalities – Italian, Spanish, Estonian, Polish, Latvian and many others – which often makes communication rather difficult, though it enriches all our experiences of community and what that means when we come from different places.

Finally, after many phone calls, and probably many hours in total spent on hold, I managed to get them help, and get them the benefits they were entitled to, though it was a soul-breaking experience.

'God, please watch over the family. Please keep the boy safe, and put food on the table and hope in their hearts. Please God, don't let them be forgotten again …' I prayed for them that night. I prayed for everyone who was struggling.

I have no idea why these things happen and why there is so much injustice, and yet I have to trust that this is all part of God's work, and God's plan. This can be extremely hard, and, at the time, it took a lot to centre myself back into my beliefs and carry on. When I feel like that, I generally take to the woods or hills with my dogs. That's where I find peace and rest when I'm walking in nature, and it helps steady me. I needed to be steadied – I had work to do for them. I had to find them much-needed furniture. I had to chase up the benefits payments. I had to do the work God had entrusted me with.

Wandering into Greggs one morning not long after, to grab a £2 bacon butty and a coffee, which had become part of my new normal, I caught sight of a man in dark glasses and clergy attire. He had a bald head and a large crucifix tattooed on his hand.

Ey up, who's this on my patch? I thought. Taking hold of my warm sandwich and my paper cup filled with scalding coffee, I went over and introduced myself.

'How are ye? I'm Father Alex; who are you?' The man looked up at me, and, without taking off his shades, replied: 'Alright, I'm Pastor Mick. I haven't seen ye before.'

'I'm the priest at St Matthew's. Where's your ministry?' I asked, taking a bite out of my butty. Pastor Mick clearly had the same idea to come here for a spot of breakfast before the work of the day commenced.

'I'm from the Church on the Street Ministries. I work with the homeless, with the poor of the community. Things are bad for the people round here, very bad, and it gets worse every day with the pandemic and the restrictions,' he said.

I had to agree.

'I'm hearin' stories of people who can't see a doctor, who have illnesses they can't get treated, and people are being laid off. It's getting worse and I worry all the time. Schoolteachers have started to ring me to tell me that the kids who can't come into school probably don't eat at home because money is so tight. It's heartbreaking,' I replied.

'It is, Father, it's heartbreaking.'

We both went our separate ways that morning, but Pastor Mick stayed in my mind, and I wasn't at all surprised to bump into him a couple of days later. God works in mysterious ways, after all. This time, we sat down and had a proper chat about what was going on in the town, and how things were getting worse. Our ministry at St Matthew's was behind the curve when it came to outreach, and I wanted to do more. Even so, it didn't occur to me where this chance meeting would take us both.

New restrictions were being rolled out by the day, it seemed, and there were new problems of economic hardship and job losses that now started to hit local families as we entered autumn and winter of 2020. Things looked very bleak. There had also been huge problems with the distribution of school meal vouchers across our area, and I had started being very vocal about this on social media. The storm clouds were gathering again, and this time it felt like a hurricane was blowing in. By now, I was angry. I was angry that as a church we had failed people at a time they'd needed us the most. I was angry that children were not getting access to meal vouchers, and were coming in to school without being fed. I was angry that people couldn't feed their kids because they'd had to stop work or lost their jobs.

The first people we helped together were the family from Europe. Mick and I did a call-out and soon people were donating furniture for them. We got them a sofa, a double bed for the parents and a television. We topped up the leccy and gave them a bit of cash to get by on until their Universal Credit arrived. They were the tip of the iceberg, as we soon discovered.

The Lord's Prayer is the prayer that teaches us how to pray. When Jesus' disciples asked him how they should pray, he taught them this. Most Christians know the prayer by heart and it is one I have always said throughout my life, years and years before becoming a Christian. It has so much meaning to me, as it asks God to watch over us; our families, communities and lives. It asks for our basic needs for sustenance to be met and it allows us to ask forgiveness for our sins. It also asks us to accept God's will for us, to ask that his will is done. This raised difficult questions when I saw the terrible circumstances the family had fallen into. It raised hard-to-answer questions when I learnt that families couldn't feed their kids because they couldn't go to school. Yet, it is not for me to try to divine God's will; that is where trust and faith come in. Often, I am called upon to explain the unexplainable, and I cannot. I am a man. I am not God. The Lord's Prayer asks us to accept God's will 'on earth as it is in heaven'. This is a tricky concept in a world obsessed with control and certainty. It is a simple prayer, though, and I have always loved it because it tells me I don't have to be top of the class or use complicated language to have access to God's love. God's will was to crucify his own Son, and, as such, it is unfathomable to me, a simple man. I try not to decipher it too much. It is not my job. It is my job to create a space for questions regarding spirituality and God's will to be asked. One thing that binds myself, Mick and all Christians together is the Lord's Prayer. It is not enough simply to acknowledge God's will, but it is essential to do God's will, to carry out God's will, to bring his kingdom to earth as he did when he sent Jesus. That will is in my and Mick's hearts as it is in that of many Christians, and it is exactly why we, for a period of time, shared a ministry together, and precisely why these stories are being shared with you in this book.

9.

IT ISN'T AN ARGOS CHRISTMAS

'For we are God's workmanship, created in
Christ Jesus to do good works, which God
prepared in advance for us to do.'

Ephesians 2:10

'It's alright, there's enough for everyone!' One of the volunteers shouted as people surged towards Pastor Mick's modest Toyota Aygo, which was stacked full of bags we'd earlier stuffed full of dry food and tins.

'Come on, there's plenty here. It isn't an Argos Christmas you know,' I added, handing out a bag to the carer of a disabled lady in a wheelchair. She was wrapped up in thin blankets but still looked cold. We had a saying during my time as a store manager: 'It isn't an Argos Christmas', which was shorthand for 'Don't panic'. It referred to the sometimes hellish experience of working at Argos during late December each year, with last-minute shoppers queuing down the street, people squabbling over games consoles or putrid-coloured Furbies, and a huge amount of pressure. The idea is that if it's not an Argos Christmas then there's nothing to worry about. I'm not sure how well this applies to people in situations like those facing the people of the parish as the winter lockdown ground on, and as the job losses hit home.

'There's hot food as well; there's plenty, don't worry. There's enough,' Pastor Mick was saying as he handed out the bags alongside donated hot dinners in polystyrene containers.

'Can I really just have a bag of food?' One man came up to me. He looked well dressed and I'd seen him earlier park up in a nice car.

'Of course. We don't means-test anyone, brother,' I said, wondering what on earth he was doing here at a pop-up foodbank. He was concerned that he might be getting something he shouldn't.

'You can have as much as you need,' I continued, handing him a bag. 'There are no forms to fill out. You don't need to be referred, it's all free and it's for you. If ye don't mind me asking, why are ye here?'

The man smiled ruefully. 'I lost my job at the start of the pandemic. The benefits don't cover my outgoings. I've got three children and I'm mortgaged to the hilt with a four-bedroom house. That's why I'm here, Father,' he said.

'I'm Father Alex, and you're always welcome. Take another bag to help ye out.'

'Thank you. I'm Graham. In the nicest possible way, I hope I'll get a new job soon and won't see you again.' I watched him go, carrying his food, the burden of his unemployment riding heavy on his shoulders.

It was a bitterly cold November night and we were parked up in a Burnley car park, with Pastor Mick's boot overflowing with food given to us by the wonderful people from those terraces and businesses around the church. The response to our appeal had been phenomenal. As we still weren't allowed to hold services or invite people into St Matthew's, we decided to work together expanding the foodbank that Mick had started in a public space so that anybody could come who needed a hot meal inside them and a bag of essentials. I'd put a message out on social media expecting a few people to turn up, but when Mick parked his car outside my vestry door, it wasn't long before people started showing up. The word had got out.

'Alright, Father Alex. Here's a dozen packets of soup and some rolls,' said one of our regular churchgoers as he walked up.

'Alright, Father Alex, I've got some tins of beans, some soup and a few tins of vegetables; just the basics but someone might be able to use them,' said another.

By the end of that day we had a dozen or so bags filled with food to hand out to local families. It was a drop in an ocean of need, but it was a start. The following week we did the same, and this time we couldn't fit all the food into Mick's car.

What started to happen was that people would come to us for food packages, and we'd get chatting. I began to learn more about the lives of people around me, their stories and their problems. The hardship around us was just unbelievable. It wasn't only financial now, it was the emotional and spiritual impact of the Covid measures that was so distressing. So many were separated from loved ones and were struggling alone. So many were unable to grieve properly or worship properly. There was a huge sense of isolation, and so they came to us. The volume of food – and people wanting it – grew each week, and so I put out another message asking for volunteers. Again, we were inundated. Soon, volunteers were helping us drive food parcels out to people who couldn't or wouldn't come to the foodbank. Many felt a huge sense of shame at having to rely on our parcels, which was so hard to see. Frequently, I delivered food to someone after dark so that the neighbours wouldn't see. Many of the older people in our community felt ashamed that they couldn't make ends meet and needed our help. I continued vocalising what I was seeing – the hardship and suffering, the turmoil and injustices the pandemic had created – on social media. Soon, we had to find a place to store the food donations and so I cleared out the choir vestry room and we put it in there. So many people came to help that I remember breaking down in tears as I realised how much food we'd been given and grasped the extent of people's kindness. I went onto my platforms and just told people how humbling it was to see this kindness in such difficult times, expressing the gratitude I felt for what people were doing for our community. I also challenged the council and the councillors who are meant to be representing us, and asked what they were doing to help. The experience lifted our spirits, and brought light into the darkness. The donations grew and grew with this deep-rooted desire in our community to help those in need.

As two ordained ministers, Mick and I could not have been more different. Mick's methods were, to me, unorthodox. He had a natural disdain for organised religion, whereas I am embedded within the structure and complex hierarchy and traditions of the Church of England. This was the national church fraternising with a free church, and we were demon-strating that we could work together and pool our resources. We became a strong voice in a unique time that may never be replicated. It did show me there is much we can do to work together with our Christian brothers and sisters. Our ministry is so different; Mick is a street pastor and serves the people on the fringes of society in a way that the state church can't. I'm responsible for a particular parish; I have the 'cure of souls', meaning the care of the people of my parish for the particular area I serve. That doesn't mean to say I don't have to care about other areas of Burnley – I do passionately care – but there are other Church of England vicars who have the responsibility for those areas. I also have other responsibili-ties. I am a school governor, and I teach the Christian faith in church schools and secular schools. I am a parish priest while Pastor Mick's ministry in the Free Church is, in many ways, rather more liberating and self-directed.

Mick was a brilliant challenge for me, as I wanted to work out how I could do what he does but in a Church of England context. Mick doesn't serve a parish, he serves a community, and therein lay some of the main differences. I have Parish Church Councils and committees that I am responsible for and accountable to. I represent the state church, which includes following Canonical obedience to my bishops and allegiance to the Queen. It means I am legally licensed to marry people in the Church of England, but sadly only if they are heterosexual. Mick serves in a much freer way so the landscape is different; we are in the same town but we are working in different arenas. The common denominator, though, was that we both have a real heart for serving the poor, in our different ways. Mick was such a blessing to me, and has enabled us both to be a blessing to the parish. Together we shared in a gospel partnership. We both saw the food crisis develop on the ground as more and more families came to us for help. All the time, I was calling out the government and the council on social media as I felt so strongly that it didn't seem right that we were having to feed people. I was asking why people weren't able to cope? Tins of beans and peas became the light in that darkness, and I wanted to know how we as a society had got to that point.

'Hi, is that Father Alex?' The voice at the end of the phone wasn't the usual accent of people around here.

'Yes, that's me. How can I help?' I said, one eye on some papers I needed to look through.

'Hi. This is Louise. I'm a producer from the BBC. We're wondering if you'd like to take part in a film we're making about the impact of the pandemic on northern towns and urban areas?'

'You what?' I mumbled, putting the documents down.

'Sorry, yes, it's BBC News; we're doing a piece with local headteachers, businesses, GPs and other stakeholders about how Covid is impacting people and we wondered if the Church would like to take part. We've heard about the work you're doing with the foodbank and we'd like to come and speak to you. Would that be possible?'

My head was flipping out.

'Er, yes, well I'll need to speak to Pastor Mick and check he's happy with that too. Thank you for your interest in us. Can I get back to ye?' I put down the phone.

'Sarah … you'll never guess who just rang …'

The next day, I chatted to Pastor Mick. We were sorting

tins for the food parcels companionably though it was freezing cold outside the vestry.

'So, what do ye think? I know it's the BBC, but I don't want to risk portraying a bad image of the town, or its people ...' I mulled over the idea as I threw in some Haribos I'd found in a cupboard indoors.

'Well, did ye speak to the bishop?' said Pastor Mick. He was wearing a thick black coat and I could see the large cross tattooed on his left hand as he worked. Pastor Mick was a reformed addict who had transformed his life from one of violence and prison into one of recovery and service to those at the bottom of society. I admired him and his ministry greatly.

'Yeah, he is supportive, saying it's about time we had some Christian witness, something in the news about Christianity doing good works. If we can get your van in with the details of your mission, and we can get my dog collar on t'telly, then job done, we're spreading the word ...'

BBC Special Correspondent Ed Thomas turned up and filmed me down at one of our schools. It was exciting, but we thought we were a small segment in a film about the wider community. Then Louise rang again.

'Actually, Father Alex, we've decided just to focus on the work you and Pastor Mick have been doing with the foodbank. Can we come back and do some more filming?'

'Blimey, well, alright then, though it was Pastor Mick who started giving out food from his car. I've just come in and helped take it to more people, but perhaps you should just do the piece on him?' I spluttered.

'Ed says he definitely wants you in it,' added Louise before hanging up. We'd agreed a date. I just had to tell my wife.

'I'm really nervous,' I started. Sarah just looked at me.

'What do you always say when it isn't a life-or-death situation?' She smiled.

'It isn't an Argos Christmas …' we both said together, and laughed.

'Alright, I'll give it a go,' I said. 'After all, I've been on *Supermarket Sweep* so I'm a seasoned telly pro.' Sarah raised her eyebrows and said nothing.

On a grim, drizzling winter day just before the BBC arrived, Pastor Mick and I were handing out food bags, this time from the vestry door of the church as we had so many donations we couldn't fit them all in Mick's car.

A woman turned up I didn't recognise, so I went over to her.

'Alright, how are ye?' I said, trying to be as un-priest-y as possible.

The woman, who looked like she'd had a hard life, just looked at me, and replied: 'Not really.'

'What's to do?' I asked, thinking it was the usual shame of having to use a foodbank. It wasn't.

'My daughter has hung herself,' she said simply.

'Your daughter's …?' I replied, stunned by this terrible news. Her words took the breath out of me.

The woman shrugged, and in that gesture I saw the hopelessness she felt, and it was that which shook me the most.

'She hung herself and I'm not allowed to go and see her because of Covid. Can't travel and she's in Preston …'

I have never felt so crap as a minister as I did then. I just did not know what to say to this woman. The depths of her suffering must've been absolute, and there I was, holding a bag of pasta and beans, trying to find the right words where there were none to be found. I wanted to help, but I didn't know how. I wanted to say the right things, but she needed me to listen. And I wanted to take the pain and hurt from her, but I couldn't.

If I'm honest, she looked haggard. She looked cold and drawn, and on top of that she was dealing with the most horrific grief.

Pastor Mick did what any compassionate human being would do and hugged her, though the restrictions told us we couldn't, while I went into the church and tried to find some treats for her food parcel, as if a few packets of custard creams could make up for the tragedy she'd suffered. We gave her an extra bag, and it was nowhere near enough in terms of helping her. It haunts me to this day because I feel that if I was being a priest properly, doing what Jesus asks of me, then I'd have broken the law, taken her into church and offered her that sacred space to talk about her feelings and her daughter. I will probably never understand why her daughter killed herself, as I never found out the mother's name – nor where she might be staying, though I suspect poverty, hardship and all the troubles associated with that may have had a part to play. I felt caught between the constraints of Covid and the enormity of what she'd shared with me. Strangely, I came away feeling that we'd offered her something that wasn't just the food parcels. She'd come to us because she needed food despite the trauma she'd suffered, and there was something very humbling in the dignity she showed. She wasn't wailing and weeping, she was almost resigned to her fate and that of her daughter. What I saw was the cycle of poverty repeating itself endlessly, with transient populations, with no fixed address, sofa surfing for somewhere to sleep, living on the fringes of society with little or no normality in their lives.

The next day, the BBC film crew arrived and set up with admirable skill and precision. We were still stunned by the woman and her daughter, and I almost said I couldn't do the interview, I felt so raw and fragile. The cameraman Phil put me at my ease, so much so that at the end of my piece, when I thought the cameras had been turned off, I burst into tears. Unbeknown to me, he'd kept the camera rolling, and in some ways I felt as vulnerable and as exposed in that moment as the people who were being forced to come to the car park must've been feeling. I was knackered from weeks of collecting donations, bagging them up and delivering them by hand, as restrictions meant we couldn't have volunteers inside the church. Many times, I'd been the only person someone had seen all day, and I was exhausted by the misery and loss.

Christmas was now on the horizon. Late one night, there was a knock at the vicarage door.

'I'll get it,' I shouted to Sarah from the hallway.

If you're a vicar then the chances are that you'll get people knocking at the door at all times of the day and night asking for money, food or help.

'Alright, what's to do?' I said to the man standing on my doorstep. He looked in a state. He was pissed, ragged-looking, and I knew he'd walked a country mile to get here because I recognised him and was aware he lived out of town. If I'm honest, he looked completely fucked.

'What ye doin' here, mate?' I said to Joe.

'Sorry to bother ye, Vicar, but I need yer help ...' he said, slurring.

'Go on, Joe, what d'ye need?'

'It's my daughter. It's her birthday and I've got nothin' to give her, Vicar. Can ye help me out?' Perhaps people might've judged him for having enough to buy beer but not enough for a present, but that's not my job.

'Ye want a present for your daughter? How old is she? I'll have to see what we've got,' I replied, as if I was Father Christmas in a dog collar. What on earth could I give a little girl I'd never met before? It's not like we kept a stash of selection boxes or gifts for moments such as this.

'She's eight … I think …' came Joe's voice. I sighed. I had a rummage round in the kitchen, hoping there might be some stray Haribos from the foodbank offerings or nice cakes, at least.

'Here ye go. It's the best I can do,' I said, handing him a box of Fox's biscuits.

It's something I hear a lot at the foodbank. 'Father Alex, it's me granddaughter's birthday, have ye got anythin'?' 'Father Alex, it's my nephew's birthday …' etc., and I am forced to scrabble about among the essentials to find something to help them out.

'Thanks, Vicar. See ye around,' Joe said and wandered off, unsteadily.

Handing out food is, for me, part of doing God's work, honouring what the verse tells us he has prepared us to do. I find it really upsetting, though, and I couldn't get that little girl and that packet of biscuits, which was her present, out of my mind for a long time.

10.

FAITH

'You know the way to the place
where I am going.'

John 14:4

'Alright, what's to do?' I said as Jenny Swears-a-Lot walked
towards me in the park. She was with one of her mates, whom
I didn't recognise.

'Am I fuck,' she replied, as usual.

'Sorry to hear that. What's happened?' I said, throwing a
stick for the dogs to chase.

'Oh, me husband's not workin' because of Covid. He's
self-employed so his money's stopped completely and I've
only got me child tax, or whatever.'

'I'm really sorry to hear that. I haven't seen ye at the foodbank?' I whistled for my dog to come over. I wanted to give
Jenny my undivided attention.

'Oh no, I'm managin'. Fair enough you can freeze
yer mortgage and what-not, so we froze all that, but we've
lost a full wage. I'm not slagging people off who are on

benefits cos I'm on them meself, but them where the money hadn't stopped, they're gettin' extra money to feed their kids, and their money hasn't changed, whereas we've lost a full wage.'

'I think people are getting top-ups?' I said, instantly concerned for Jenny and her family.

'Yeah, I think ye get what you normally get in school dinners, £11 or what-not, I don't know, but they're getting that a week per child in Asda or Tesco vouchers. So, for instance, one of me friends has five kids, so she's gettin' something like sixty-odd pounds a week on top of the money she already has,' Jenny said.

'How does that make ye feel?'

'I just thought, "What?" I'm not just saying me, but there must be other self-employed people who're in proper dire straits. Luckily, I've the kids' tax credits money and me mum gets me bits and stuff, so we're alright. But there must be people who've nothing.'

'I'm sure you're right. I still don't know how the hell you're coping,' I added. The sky was starting to darken as twilight set in, though there were still plenty of people about walking their dogs.

'Don't get me wrong, we still have some money with benefits and that. I don't begrudge anyone getting any money, but I just think sometimes, some people get a lot more out than what other people get.'

'Some people just fall through the gaps, don't they?'

'Yeah. I didn't want any extra money, but if I'd just got a top-up so I could get the kids some dinners or whatever. It's hard, as obviously I just have me child tax and I've got to find council tax and food with that.' Jenny seemed as upbeat as ever even though what she was telling me was pretty hard to hear.

'Have ye got enough?' I asked.

'Well, you scrimp and borrow it, don't ye,' she answered. Her friend stayed quiet, nodding now and again.

'I've borrowed some money off me mum and that. It weren't much. So, I'll go shopping and me mum'll go shopping, and she'll try and match the same stuff, and she'll say, "I'll buy this for ye, Jenny," so luckily she's helpin' out. I'm able to get the amount of food to feed us all.'

'That's quite an achievement to feed seven of you, Jenny,' I said, shaking my head with absolute wonder. Neither woman was complaining really. They took life on the chin. I'd almost say they had faith that everything would somehow work out. I went home, thinking I would write my sermon for the following Sunday about faith, as it was such a necessary commodity in these straitened times.

In November 2020, the documentary was aired on the 6pm and 10pm BBC News programmes. We watched it as a family in the dining room. Sarah turned to me and whispered, 'That was powerful.' I felt very sombre afterwards, but what followed was nothing short of extraordinary. My mobile started to ring. Then again. And again. Then, the landline started. Calls were coming in one after the other, all asking for Father Alex, all offering food, money, donations, people's time – and I later discovered that Mick was receiving the same.

We were asked to appear on BBC Radio 5 Live, and on the *Jeremy Vine* show; we were approached by the *Guardian* newspaper to do a feature; and the calls kept on coming. For the next 24 hours, my daughter Holly became my Personal

Assistant, fielding calls and telling people how to donate. The next morning, I rang the diocese and asked for some help, and they provided me with a PA for about a week. Huge amounts of money began pouring in to St Matthew's from donors all over the country and the world. That night, just as I was lowering my testicles into a steaming hot bath, the Archbishop of York rang and I had one of the most bizarre conversations of my life. He asked me if it was a good time to call. 'I'm actually stark naked, Your Grace.'

'I just wanted you to know that the work you and Pastor Mick are doing reminded me why I became a priest.' If that wasn't surreal enough, I received a call the next morning that floored me.

'May I speak to Father Alex?' the voice at the other end of the line said in a posh cut-glass accent.

'Yes, that's me. How can I help?' I replied, wondering who it was this time. Perhaps it was someone offering another container-load of rice like one caller from South Africa the night before. The cut-glass accent replied: 'This is the office of the Duchess of York, Sarah Ferguson, and we'd like to help. What can we do?'

Naturally, I thought the call was a wind-up, so I said: 'You're alright, thanks, we've got everything. Goodbye,' and I put the phone down. Several seconds later it rang again and it was the same woman.

'No, I'm sorry but that won't do,' said Sarah Ferguson's private secretary. 'Sarah wants to help.' It turned out it was, in fact, the Duchess of York, and she did, in fact, want to help. I couldn't have been more mortified. Through her charity, Sarah Ferguson was as good as her word, and sent 500 parcels of gifts for the children on the estates. And the phone calls weren't just coming from the esteemed and wealthy. Little old ladies were ringing in and asking was it really that bad up North? The weekend after the news item was aired, people arrived from all over the country, queuing in their cars around the block, to bring supplies and food. One guy drove up from Watford with a car full of food, and I couldn't help but wonder if there wasn't a foodbank closer to home that could've benefited, but of course, all donations were gratefully received. All of this felt like our faith had been rewarded with proof of the kindness of strangers. That BBC film went on to be viewed millions of times, and won both the Sandford St Martin Award for Religious Broadcasting in 2021, and then the Royal Television Society Award in 2022, yet we didn't feel we were doing anything extraordinary. We felt God was in the process, though. At times, however, I confided in Mick that I didn't know whether to keep going and do things that involved publicity, and he always said the same thing to me.

'Just keep walking through the doors, Alex. Just keep walking.'

We never forgot the message underlying that documentary, which was that Covid hit the poorest the hardest. The figures make uncomfortable reading. Deaths were up 60 per cent on pre-Covid levels in our area, and the BBC report said that you were twice as likely to die of Covid if you were poor. The highest mortality rates in the UK were in the North West and North East* with the highest in the North East. The Northern

* https://www.gov.uk/government/publications/covid-19-reported-sars-cov-2-deaths-in-england/covid-19-confirmed-deaths-in-england-to-28-february-2022-report.

Health Science Alliance, which includes universities and NHS Trusts, commissioned a study into Covid 19 and the impact on the North, and the results were shocking. It found that death rates were 17 per cent higher in the North, while care-home mortality was up 24 per cent compared to the rest of the country. People in the North spent an average of 41 days more in lockdown than anywhere else in the UK, that's 41 more days in isolation, unable to work and earn an income. The report showed that wages fell in the North compared to the rest of the country, and the unemployment rate was 19 per cent higher than the rest of the UK. Prescriptions for anti-depressants soared, and there was a larger drop in mental wellbeing. No shit, Sherlock.

What the North needs isn't just a Westminster-led agenda of Levelling Up; we need to level the playing field full stop. We need better jobs for people so they can provide better lives for their families. We need decent public transport so that people can travel to work, and expand their abilities to go out and make a decent living. We need increased mental health provision for the NHS so that people here who have taken the brunt of the Covid restrictions can get better and come out the other side with the right support. We need benefits that sustain embattled families, where they aren't required to wait weeks for their money. We need proper funding for our infrastructure and for our hospitals. What these statistics tell us is that many deaths were preventable. This is a huge trag-edy for the North, and our politicians need to be asking hard-hitting questions of central government. There has been – and continues to be – real despair here. We are talking about people's lives, people who hurt, and bleed, and cry – and very often I cry along with them. The work of the Church and local charities is keeping many in the community alive, yet it isn't enough. Children have lost parents. Rates of suicide have increased. I know this is an opportunity to live out the gospel in serving the poor and helping the needy, yet the daily injustice wears me down. As people weep, I truly believe God weeps as well.

'So, I'm ready to announce Tin of the Week ... Drum roll please ...' I shouted above the din, as volunteers milled about outside the church, bagging up supplies and chatting. There was a general cheer from everyone, and it was quite a comical sight as they were all wearing Volunteer sweatshirts, the kind I used to order for my staff at Argos to encourage team spirit.

'Wooooooooooo ... And this week, the most interesting donation award goes to ... a tin of Bamboo Shoots!' This received rapturous applause. If only my sermons got the same reaction.

'Last week it was chicken korma; the Lord himself only knows what delights might come in next week ...'

I stepped down from the chair I'd been standing on. We were grateful for all our donated supplies, but it tended to get very same-y for our hard-up families. Each week they'd receive a bag of pasta, rice, some tinned spaghetti or baked beans, long-life milk, cheap soup, some biscuits and a jar of coffee if they got lucky.

There was humour among the recipients too. I often heard people saying: 'So, what will ye knock up this week?' knowing they'd be 'knocking up' the same as last week, and the week before that.

I can't stress enough that the impact of higher inflation, the rise in the cap on energy bills and the increased cost of food and fuel is heaping fuel on the fire created by Covid. We already have people coming to us asking for hot food because they cannot afford to heat it up at home. But I don't want our community to rely on us for food. We aren't a bottomless pit of support, and I want to be able to support in ways that have longevity beyond being able to eat well in one week. I don't get any personal satisfaction from running a foodbank, apart from the opportunity it gives me to interact with the people of my community. In fact, I detest the fact it exists at all. It shows me we've got things wrong in the wider world. It shows me our values aren't right. Our spiritual values aren't there if we keep people poor enough to be unable to buy food or hygiene supplies each week. I don't remember there being a need for foodbanks when I was a kid. I might be wrong, but they feel like a modern invention, and cater for as many working families as they do for homeless individuals. They are normalised now. They are part of the fabric of society, and I don't think I'm alone in being horrified by this. Here in Burnley, we are one of five or six foodbanks, all giving out an extraordinary amount of food. You might argue we have a community of freeloaders or 'benefit scum', as the tabloids might say, but I don't believe that's true at all. We have people who now donate to the bank when once they needed to use it themselves. At the height of the pandemic, I put a box outside the vicarage filled with tins of soup and a sign saying that if people needed it, to take it. They all went that day, then a few days later a young woman appeared at my front door. She had a buggy with a young toddler in and was crying.

'What's the matter? Can I help?' I said, bemused. She handed me the bag with most of the tins of soup still inside it.

'Don't ye need them?'

'Yeah,' she replied, 'but I took all the soups, and I should've just taken one. I just wanted to know if ye can forgive me?'

'Don't be silly!' I replied. 'If you need all the soup, take all the soup!' It took me a while to persuade her to be on her way with the food, even though I could see she was probably short of a bob or two.

Faith is a difficult concept at the best of times. Having faith in God is something that changes and shifts for me but always remains. Having faith in humankind – politicians, benefit agencies, government departments – can be downright impossible, except when I come across people like that young mum who felt bad at taking freely offered soup. The verse from John 14:4, 'You know the way to the place where I am going', concerns Jesus talking about the way to salvation being through faith in him, and so the way to heaven is through faith and faith alone. At this point Jesus knew he was facing crucifixion, and so he was preparing his disciples for events that would shortly unfold. Jesus is telling us he is the way and the truth and the life. These words are important to both people of faith and people of no faith. If you believe in Jesus, you understand that role-modelling Jesus is the way, it is the truth and it is a way of life. If you believe that the story of Jesus is a load of bollocks, then fair enough, but you are probably still trying to live a decent life.

II.

GRIEF

'... a time to be born and a time to die ...'

Ecclesiastes 3:2, 'A Time for Everything'

'Is that Father Alex?'

'Yes, it's me. How can I help?' I replied one sunny spring day after the end of the second lockdown. I had just written my sermon for Sunday's service and was humming to myself as I answered the phone.

'It's the undertaker. It's a tricky one this is, Alex.' Inwardly, I sighed.

'You always say that. What is it this time?' I asked.

'A young father took his own life,' the undertaker said. 'He left behind three children. Can you go and see the widow?'

'Of course. Send me over the details,' I replied, my heart swooping down into my stomach. The family lived on a nearby estate just west of the town centre. It wasn't too far to walk so I set off. The day had dawned quite bright and I was grateful for that at least. I knew this visit would not be a comfortable one.

'Alright, Father Alex,' said a man I knew back in my Argos days as I walked along the concrete roads and pathways. Though there is countryside within minutes of the centre, there wasn't much in the way of trees or planting to interrupt the convenience stores, rows of fatigued-looking council properties, off-licences, bookies and general neglect of the area. Perhaps it's worth mentioning just how many bookies there are in Burnley, especially dotted around the two main estates of Stoops and Griffin. Where there is deprivation and poverty, there are bookies and off-licences aplenty, or so it seemed to me that morning. I wondered what I was about to walk into.

'Are ye alright?' I said in reply to the man, a guy who'd done quite well at the retailer, from memory. He looked chipper, so I smiled and we carried on walking along our different paths. I found the house at last. It was a typical corporation home, a boxy pale-coloured terrace with a smattering of windows and a small patch of grass in the yard out front. I knocked and the door opened to reveal a woman who looked wretched. She was a forlorn-looking figure in her doorway.

'Hello, I'm Father Alex. I've come to see ye. Can I come in?' I said, my heart already weeping for her.

'Of course, Father, come in,' she replied, and I followed her down the corridor to the back room, which had a table and chairs, was very clean, and had cushions and some decoration. This wasn't the typical sort of house I was used to entering. It was obvious this lady took pride in her home and there were nice curtains and wallpaper on the walls.

As she made us a brew, I kept asking myself: 'Is this woman ready to see me?' It's a difficult question to answer. She was in the eye of the hurricane with her grief, that much was already obvious, but it is a really important part of the grief process to move forward little by little, and plan the funeral.

'Here ye go, Father,' she said, bustling back with a couple of nice china cups on a tray, and a plate of Bourbons.

'Thank you,' I answered, picking up a biscuit and dunking it in my brew.

We both sipped our drinks companionably. My instincts told me to wait and listen to whatever she felt she wanted to say. I was her witness, for as long as she needed me that morning.

'I had no idea he felt the way he did. He didn't let anything show,' she began at last.

'I'm really sorry I have to be here in these terrible circumstances,' I replied softly, 'and I'm here to help in whatever way I can.'

'Thank ye. I can't fathom why he did it,' she continued. 'He always seemed so happy, so loving towards the kids ... I just don't know how I'm feeling; it must be the shock.'

'How are your children?' I asked.

'Well, they're grown up now, of course. My eldest boy is away at college, and my two girls are teenagers, but they miss him. We all do ...' Tears started running down the woman's face. She wiped them away. She was a kind-looking lady who was quite well dressed and who looked like someone who worked hard.

'Of course ye do. Tell me a little bit about your husband,' I said, hoping in talking about him she might draw some comfort from his memory.

She put her cup down and looked at me. There were dark shadows under her eyes and they looked red and puffy. She looked like she hadn't slept for days.

'I don't know what to tell ye. He had a good job working as a lorry driver, but he loved spending time down at Turf Moor and with the kids. Terry and our son Jon would go to the matches together. They were passionate Burnley fans. He loved the footie. He had his mates and they'd go for a pint afterwards, but he was a quiet man, a family man. He doted on the girls. I just had no idea. I had no idea, Father ... I know I've got to do this. I've got to organise his funeral and get things goin', but I don't know how to carry on ...'

I gave her a small smile.

'I understand. Grief isn't easy, and you're right, things do need to move on for everyone's sake and this can feel very hard in the first few days and weeks after a loved one has passed,' I told her.

'I just feel so guilty, Father. What if there was somethin' I could've done that would've stopped this from happening? What if there was somethin' I missed? I don't think I'll ever forgive meself,' she answered. The tears started again and she got up and went to get a tissue.

I remembered when I worked at Argos, one day a man approached me and asked to speak with me. I said, 'Of course.'

'I've noticed the cross ye wear on your suit jacket, and I'm assumin' you're goin' to be a priest?'

I nodded. 'Yes, I am.'

'I've never told anyone this, but my son killed himself. I found him swinging from a tree at the bottom of the garden. The worst thing was, we didn't realise he felt so bad. We didn't know to help him ...' The employee looked at me, and I understood he needed a witness to his pain and his suffering.

'I'm sorry to hear that,' I said simply.

As a priest I can't give people any answers. I don't know why their loved ones choose to end their lives rather than carry on living. I don't know why people choose to kill themselves, but I can say that I've skirted pretty close to depression in some parts of my life, so I have a small understanding of the sense of despair that might push someone into this action. I'm constantly asked to explain the unexplainable, and to give comfort where there may be little to give, yet I will never give up trying to bring some peace to people suffering the tragedy of a loved one's death.

I wasn't meant to be in that lady's house that day. The pandemic restrictions were back in place and so I knew very well I was breaking the law by going into the bereaved woman's home. Perhaps I should be given a fine like the ones handed out to the government for the Downing Street parties during lockdown. Perhaps I deserve one as much as those who drank Prosecco and celebrated whatever it was they were celebrating. I don't care. If I had my time, I would do it again. I couldn't Zoom call that woman to chat about her husband's suicide. That, to me, would've been utterly heartless, so I made the choice to go around and speak to her as a human being, to acknowledge her pain in the flesh. Despite this, I had to work out a way to give this lady a funeral her husband deserved. He was a well-loved member of the community, and at the time we were only allowed to have a small number of mourners inside the crematorium. I liaised with the undertaker and we decided to hold the service outside at Burnley Cemetery because this felt like quite a significant death. All deaths are significant, but we knew, for this one, there would be many from the community who might wish to come along and pay their respects.

We arranged for the funeral service to take place at the graveside, something I've never done before or since. People were still having to stand two metres apart, so when the crowds wandered in, they were dotted in family clumps. It reminded me of going to big festivals and standing at one of the lesser stages, with people here and there, milling about in small groups. It wasn't a festival, of course, though somebody did turn up with a large speaker and a microphone so I could be heard by everybody. I conducted the service in torrential rain. Someone had to stand by me holding an umbrella over me as I did the readings. We couldn't stay too long because of the weather, but the rain seemed to echo the deep sense of loss that was openly felt by this large group of people.

Funerals during Covid were terrible. I cannot think of a more sterile way of holding one than with a small number of permitted mourners wearing masks and standing two metres apart from each other. Often, I would barely recognise the immediate family of the deceased as their faces were covered. It was taking longer to bury or cremate people because of all the measures. It created some awkward, and strangely humorous, situations.

One time, I was asked by a family member to go and say prayers with the deceased person. The undertaker rang me.

'You shouldn't really be coming. The lid needs to go on.'

'Ah, I see,' I replied. 'The family wants me to come in, so I think I'll have to ...'

I arrived at the undertakers and a man, probably in his fifties, greeted me.

'I'm sorry for your loss,' I murmured as he walked me into the room where the body was laid out.

'Hello Mum, this is Father Alex.'

I looked over at the body, half expecting her to reply. I could tell she needed to be put away as there was the slight odour of decay though her face looked as fine as it could do, with her being dead of course. The son looked at me, and for a moment I panicked.

'Should I say "Hello" back?' I asked, genuinely confused. He looked at me, puzzled.

'No, Father, she's dead.'

What did I think I would say to her anyway? Nice weather we're having? How are you keeping? It's time to get you in the ground?

Death is still treated as a taboo subject in our society, yet it is a natural part of life. Some funerals I have taken since the restrictions eased have been a joy and a true celebration of much-loved members of the community.

When the first chords of 'The Wonder of You' by Elvis Presley rang out in the church, I instinctively asked everyone to stand.

'Come on, let's wave our arms together,' I said, which isn't exactly in the funeral rites. There wasn't a moment's hesitation. The mourners who had been laughing and crying during the service, one sunny summer day, all stood up. As the song carried on, we all sang and swayed with our arms in the air. I didn't know whether to laugh or cry, it was such a powerful, beautiful, eccentric moment.

Afterwards, as I stood at the door, shaking everyone's hands as we were now allowed to do, the family came over. They'd lost a much-loved father and grandfather, but it was as joyful a funeral as I'd ever taken. There had been so much love shown in the church that day.

'Thank ye, Father, that were magic,' said his daughter, Verity.

'Yes, thank ye, I think Grandpa would've enjoyed that service. It was a proper send-off,' someone else beamed. That was a relief! I felt like I'd nailed it as the service continued but you can never be sure, particularly doing something as crazy as swaying to an Elvis song. The fact they'd loved it, and I'd sensed I could do that and make it fun, was a real Bruce-y Bonus for me. It was a great feeling, seeing the mourners go away still laughing and smiling. What a brilliant tribute to their loved one.

My favourite funeral might've been one where I was asked to do a tribute to the deceased's favourite comedians, Morecambe and Wise, by doing their funny walk down the aisle at the end of the service. The stand-up comic inside me was thrilled to be asked, and it was great fun, though I am always keenly aware that the Christian message should not be overshadowed amid the larks. Saying that, some of the funerals I've presided over haven't been so much fun as an excuse for a punch-up. I've had bouncers on the church doors to keep some of the mourners from getting lairy, and one time a family actually kicked off and had a fist fight outside the church. Thankfully, moments like that don't happen too often, but when they do, all hell breaks loose.

'Father Alex, there's a fight outside the church!' Reverend Kat, my training incumbent, a lovely lady who is in a same-sex relationship and training to be a priest, came hurrying into the vestry.

'I thought they might kick off,' I replied, sighing. 'There's not a lot we can do except wait to see if they calm down enough for the service to take place,' I said, not at all sure how to proceed. Reverend Kat and I stayed back to see what would happen, and thankfully the commotion died down quickly and I was able to do the service, though it was a bit nerve-racking, wondering if there would be more upset and offence taken during the readings. Afterwards, Kat and I sat and had a brew together. She had only recently joined the church after the bishop had asked if I felt happy taking on a trainee in a civil partnership. I didn't hesitate.

'Come and walk around the estates with me and see how ye feel about coming here,' I said to Kat on the phone, wanting her to know what she might be getting herself into.

'I'd like that,' she replied.

'Oh, and bring walking boots,' I added. We were going to pound the pavements together. On a chilly autumnal day, Kat and her partner Esther joined me and my dogs on a tour of the local area. I have to say, Burnley didn't look its best that day.

'That'll be the cannabis ye can smell,' I grinned as we began our walk. Kat was a reserved lady, a good twenty years or so younger than me, with a gentle manner. Tall and slim, she strode beside me with her wife.

'I don't mind that. It's everywhere these days, isn't it,' she said.

'Oops, mind the dog shit,' I added, swerving out of its way, while she did the same.

'This isn't Mayfair, if ye know what I mean, but this community has real heart and soul. I wouldn't want to leave here because it gets under your skin, the people get under your skin,' I mused as we walked.

It was one of those days when everyone we passed seemed to know me.

'Alright, Father Alex.'

'How are ye, Father Alex?'

'That was a lovely sermon on Sunday, Father Alex.'

'My piles are playin' me up somethin' terrible, Father Alex ...'

And so it went on.

'Watch out for the Rottweiler at the next house. He looks vicious and he'll make a run for the gate, but he should be chained up so you're not in any real danger,' I said. Sure enough, a snarling hound lurched at the gate as we passed. I sneaked a glance over at this woman who was considering joining St Matthew's. Kat seemed undaunted.

By the time we got to Subway for a posh butty, she was nodding at Esther and smiling.

'I want to come. I can see there's good work to be done here, and I can see there is community here, so if you'll take me, I'd like to carry on my training with you,' she said.

I'd just bitten into my Chicken Teriyaki sandwich.

Swallowing, I replied: 'Listen, don't decide straight away, it's a big decision. Let's speak later and if you'd still like to come then I'd be delighted.'

I could see immediately that Kat and I had very different personalities. She is highly intelligent, while I'm prone to error at every turn. I'm constantly putting my foot in it so I decided we'd make a good team. I drew on my Argos management background, which was all about working collaboratively, and using each team member's different strengths. If there were two Father Alexes – as both manager and deputy – it would be a catastrophe.

Reverend Kat rang me a couple of days later and her decision was the same. She joined our church and we've been a great team. I'm utterly unconcerned about her sexuality, as I imagine she is about mine. I only care about whether we are good clerics, serving the people we should be serving.

Back in that funeral, the fight dissipated and we got through the service together. Grief does strange things to people. Emotions run high, and people act in ways that may not represent who they are. The closest way I can describe my own grief when my dad died is to say it felt like the bad bout of Covid I suffered. My head was foggy, my brain felt like it didn't work properly and even the simplest things over-whelmed me. The intensity of the feelings of loss would come in waves, in peaks and troughs rather than being something that was static or stayed the same. There were times when making a cup of tea felt exhausting and difficult, while walk-ing in the garden seemed impossible. People often ask me if my faith got me through that time, and of course it did, but I'm also human and it didn't change the sense of loss I expe-rienced. I do know that it's easier to walk through a rite of passage, like losing a loved one, when you have faith, when, as a Christian, you believe that they have begun another jour-ney somewhere else. I believe he is with God, and because of that, I have never taken flowers to my dad's grave because I know he's not there. It is my view that when we're dead in this life, we're dead. Perhaps it's a northern thing, but we have a pragmatism that says you only die once in this world. I cannot understand but I empathise when people put flowers and teddies on lampposts after a fatal crash, because the way I see it their loved one is simply not there. It becomes a shrine, but to what? To me, it's illogical, but I also recognise that to others, it's deeply therapeutic.

I walk my dogs every day, and often I pass through the local cemetery. I was up there recently and a song by Dolly Parton was blasting out of a car radio. I looked over and there was a gathering at someone's graveside.

'Let's play it loud so she can hear it,' one of the mourners said loudly.

Obviously, they meant the woman who was buried underground and not the American singer, but it made me smile. The grieving process is different for everyone. I don't believe that the soul or spirit of a person is contained where they were buried or cremated, but that is because, as a Christian, it is my heartfelt belief that our souls begin a new life with Our Heavenly Father.

The helplessness I felt when I listened to the grieving mum who'd lost her husband to suicide also reminded me of one of the first times I went to see a bereaved family, not long after my installation as vicar. To make matters worse, it was a stillborn child, and the mother had to give birth to the baby knowing it had died inside her. What training can ever prepare a person to step into that situation? Certainly not the Death and Dying module, which we undertook as part of our training into the priesthood. We visited an undertaker who showed us how the coffins were made, and where the bodies were laid out, but it didn't tell us what to say, how to feel or how to serve someone who has been through the death of a baby, and will now have to face the funeral of their beloved child, with a coffin the size of my arm-span.

What on earth am I doing here? Why did I agree to this? I can't help this family, I have no clue what I'm doing here. God, what will I say to this mother, this family? How can I possibly presume what you mean by taking away their baby?

Help me, please God, help me … These were the thoughts running through my frantic mind as I walked into Burnley Hospital all those years ago. I'd answered a call from the hospital, and was now regretting ever picking up the receiver.

'Is that Father Alex?' the voice had said.

'It is. How can I help?' I replied, swallowing my mouthful of toast.

'It's the hospital chaplain. I really need help. I have to be with a family this morning, but there's another that needs a clergyman there. I'm afraid it isn't good news. The baby passed away, and the grieving family would like a priest to go and visit them.'

I hesitated, not at all sure I was up to the job. I had never been out to see a family going through anything like this, and I was new at the job.

'Of course, I'll go,' I replied, my heart pounding. I don't think I've ever felt as nervous as I did that day, parking my car and walking into Burnley General Hospital. I found my way to the antenatal ward where the family was kept in a special private room away from the wailing, very alive, babies and new mothers.

I wish in some ways I'd stopped to breathe, to take a moment before going in, but I was flustered and desperately hoping I wouldn't fuck it up and make the situation worse by saying something stupid. Modern-day priests are real people, and we are affected by the things we do, the people we see, just like anybody else. Situations can be just as uncomfortable, just as emotional, just as frightening or troubling.

I knocked at the door and a man, presumably the father, opened it.

'Come inside, Father,' he said.

There was a little basket in that room. Inside that basket was a tiny baby, laid out with its woolly hat on and its face scrunched up looking as if it were just sleeping, just like any other child, except this one would never breathe its first breath. I swallowed and found no words were coming to me. I could feel my body begin to shake and I had the sudden urge to turn tail and run. I didn't, of course. Instead, I walked in and went straight to the mother who was lying on the bed, with the basket by her side. Various family members were sitting around, ashen-looking, eyes sore from crying. I tried to look anywhere else but at the child, but found I could not.

'She's beautiful, isn't she, Father?' the mother said, her hand resting gently on the baby's tiny head.

Finally, I spoke. 'She's beautiful,' I agreed, 'and I'm just so sorry I have to be here at all. I'm deeply sorry for your loss, and for what you've been through. Have ye given her a name?'

'She's called Rebecca, Father. Thank ye for comin', it means a lot to us all ...' The woman started to cry, and I couldn't blame her. I was welling up as well.

Just then, an older woman, the grandmother, spoke. As she did so, she pushed forward a young boy of perhaps seven or eight years old. He was pale-faced and had been crying.

'Would ye be able to explain to him why his sister was taken, Father?'

For a moment, I was blind-sided. I speak about death and resurrection each Easter at our schools, in assemblies throughout Burnley. It's never an easy topic to discuss, yet there is always a message of hope in the Easter story, hope that I was finding hard to find here.

'Well, I can try,' I said. 'As Christians, we believe that when a person, or a baby like Rebecca, dies, they go to somewhere called heaven.'

'What's heaven like?' the boy asked.

'That's a very good question, and I have to give you the same answer that I was given a long time before I became a priest. I don't know, I haven't been there.' It was the same thing Reverend Richard said to me during our discussions at his vicarage many years earlier.

'We believe that the soul joins with God and begins a beautiful new journey. We believe they may not be here now but they are alive somewhere else, beginning a new path of eternal life with Jesus looking after them. I believe that Rachel is in a place now where she's well, she's cared for and she's going to live a joyful life, just in another place.'

The boy nodded. I looked up and caught the grandmother's eye. She smiled sadly, and I realised it was time for me to go, to leave them to their thoughts. I also knew I was going to break down, so I left, but, in my confusion, I couldn't find my way out of the hospital. I took the wrong lift as the sadness and anguish hit me, and had to ask a security guard to get me out. I got into my car and I am not ashamed to say I wept and wept. It was a sobering entry into my incumbency as the vicar, and for a while afterwards I wondered if I was really cut out for it.

I often wonder what it is I am actually offering a grieving family. I can't ease their burden of grief. I can't ease their suffering, except to say a few prayers. All I can ever do is listen and empathise, and perhaps act as a witness to this most traumatic event in people's lives. I offer prayers in their moments of loss and I try not to hear myself coming out with platitudes. At times like that, I have to stop and ask myself as a human being, is this true? Is what I am saying true, for me as well as them? Am I saying what I think or what I want to think?

Death is easier to rationalise if, like my granny, the person is 101 years old and they fall asleep in their chair. But when it is a precious little baby, which is meant to be embarking upon life, then what? It becomes challenging. The words of one of my favourite Depeche Mode songs kept going through my head as I wept in my car. Words are very unnecessary. And they were unnecessary. There was nothing I could say that could make that family's life better in that moment, and I knew it. I didn't want to make the situation worse by saying something empty or meaningless. I was given some good advice by an undertaker during my training. He said I would do hundreds of funerals and deal with lots of death, and I'd forget the majority of those people, but they would never forget me as the vicar who presided over their loved one's ceremony.

What a privilege, though. There are very few people in the world who experience the privilege of being invited to walk a few steps with a grieving family. There is a passage in John 14:1–4, which recounts the story of Doubting Thomas. Thomas didn't quite believe that heaven existed. Jesus actually says very little in the Bible about heaven, but he responds to this doubt by saying:

My Father's house has many rooms; if that were not so, would I have told you that I am going there to prepare a place for you. And if I go and prepare a place for you, I will come back and take you to be with me that you also may be where I am. You know the way to the place where I am going … I am the way and the truth and the life. No one comes to the Father except through me.

That tells me I cannot select only the deaths of the 101-year-olds. If I am a committed Christian, then I must take on board Jesus' message, I must be inclusive of every situation and person, no matter how challenging. It tells me there is a place in heaven, in one of the rooms in God's mansion, for me and for everyone.

It seems to me that our experience of grief and death has been fundamentally changed by the pandemic. How people grieved, and how we could give pastoral care, were decimated by the measures put in place. I believe their emotional impact has yet to be processed. When someone loses a loved one, the natural inclination for their nearest and dearest is to put their arms around that person. As a priest, it is to sit with them, be with them, share their pain for however long they need me to. For a while, that process was completely wiped out for families, clergy, funeral celebrants and undertakers. The consequences of this removal of pastoral support will surely continue to be felt across society for months and maybe years to come.

During the lockdowns, the pastoral support was completely removed and I could not support my parishioners through their process of grief. From that initial contact, to the arrival at the crematorium, the personal touches that mean so much – a handshake, a gentle hand on someone's arm, a huge hug – all of that was removed. Inside the crematorium, which used to be a lovely warm cosy place, it is now scrubbed and bleached. The lectern is scrubbed with disinfectant, the chairs look like they've been sanded down, they've been cleaned so much. The soul of the process has changed – and, in my view, it has been extremely damaging for people in my community.

There was no personal touch allowed, not even a handshake. We don't realise how important something is until we lose it.

Families weren't able to grieve properly. They weren't able to be comforted, or give comfort. Memories weren't able to be shared. The services were short. I'd say the words, say the prayers, the commendation and committal to God and then we'd leave. We weren't even allowed to stand at the door.

Death – and the rites and traditions of it – is one of the pillars of ministry. There is a saying within the clergy that we 'hatch, match and dispatch', meaning we do baptisms, weddings and funerals. They're the three pivotal parts of a Christian's life. As a priest, I have a very different thought process around death than I would have had prior to being ordained. For a Christian, death is something to be celebrated as part of the richness of life. I feel that, as a priest, I have a responsibility, obviously with great tact, empathy and compassion, to convey that in some way. We believe that it is not the end of the journey. Death is a continuation to something that is far greater than we could possibly imagine on earth. I often talk about this at funerals; the promise of eternal life is a promise of a life without the things we dislike here. There is no pain nor suffering in heaven. There is no poverty. There is no invasion of Ukraine. Simply put, heaven is paradise.

There's something really useful in thinking about death and resurrection as metaphors for life. Sometimes, we have to leave things behind for something new to begin. This can be extraordinarily painful, such as breakdown in relationships or the loss of a job. In church, I talk about it as part of God's purpose for us, for things to end so that something new is created. The estates exist almost in a bubble of their own, separate from the rest of society, with their own codes and traditions. This is never more obvious than when a death touches the whole of the estate. It's almost as if the injustices are felt together. If somebody is hurt, then they're all hurt. If one person dies, then they all suffer. I think that's unique to the estates. These are people who often have nothing. They have less than nothing in some cases, so what do they have? They have people. They have their families and loved ones. There's strength in this way of life as well as poverty and deprivation. If you need a car exhaust, somebody within the estate can sell you one. They wheel and deal together. I've never felt threatened walking around these streets. I love it that they treat me no differently from anyone else, with no airs or graces. They say it as it is. They tell you straight. They're nothing if not authentic, and they can see right through you if you're not. That's what I love about Burnley.

12.

TRANSFORMATION

'If you can? said Jesus,
everything is possible for one who believes'

Mark 9:23

I couldn't believe it. I could swear that was Joe lifting his daughter up as she giggled in the sunshine. I walked over.

'Joe, is that really you?' I smiled.

The man turned to me, and it was indeed. It was the man who had, months earlier, knocked at my door begging for a gift to give to his daughter. The man who had been shaking and stinking of cheap booze was transformed. He looked completely unlike the wretch who'd presented himself at my door that cold winter night. He had no stubble and was wearing good jeans and a clean hoodie.

'Alright, Vicar. How are ye?' he asked.

'I'm great, but I want to know what's happened to you. You look amazing! You look well and happy,' I beamed.

'I got meself into drug and alcohol treatment, Vicar, and I got clean.' He shrugged.

This time I was delighted to see him shrug. It was no big deal to him perhaps, but to me it was like a shining beacon of joy and hope.

'Well, congratulations, Joe. I'm so happy to see ye look so well. Come by the vicarage any time for a brew,' I said, knowing he probably wouldn't.

I walked out of the park that day feeling about a hundred pounds lighter. Recovery really was possible, and I'd seen the proof. I'd seen other addicts come out of treatment and get well for a while. Many slipped back into their using life, but not all, and I knew that for the lucky few this could really work, and they'd have a chance at life.

I couldn't help but think of my friend Mark. He'd appeared at church with abscesses on his hands, but he refused to let me take him to hospital.

'I'm alright, Father,' he'd said, slurring.

'You're not alright, Mark. You're far from it,' I replied, scowling. He looked a state but that was normal.

'I want to ring Social Services and report you as a vulnerable adult. Will ye let me do that?' I asked, knowing what the answer would be. 'That way, you might get some help with your circumstances ...'

'I'm alright, Father Alex. I keep meself goin'. I don't want no busy-bodies stickin' their noses in. I'm alright.'

I sighed.

He'd disappeared for a few weeks after that, but when he returned he just looked so ill that I made a decision. I couldn't let the situation carry on as it had so far. Something needed to change. I didn't know if I was doing the right thing, in fact it went against protocol again, but I got on the phone. I rang every service I could think of: the council,

Social Services, Housing. Eventually I found someone who knew Mark.

'Hello, it's Father Alex here from St Matthew's Church in Burnley. I've got a very vulnerable guy here called Mark, who really needs help. His accommodation sounds very unsafe, and he often appears at church with injuries and bruises. He's a chronic alcoholic and he needs help,' I said to the service.

'Mark? Yes, we know who ye mean. There's nothin' we can really do. He's a bit of a lost cause ...' the voice at the other end of the telephone said.

I had to pause a minute to make sure I understood what this person was saying.

'You're saying he's a lost cause? What does that mean?' I almost spluttered in sudden anger and disbelief. 'Does that mean you won't help him rather than you can't help him?'

'I'm really sorry. Mark is probably goin' to die, and we just can't do anythin' to help him. He has been resistant to our help. Is there anythin' else I can help ye with?'

I almost slammed down the phone in horror.

Mark had been written off and that wasn't good enough for me, it wasn't something I was just going to accept. The services might have failed Mark and those like him, but I was determined that the Church wouldn't. I had an idea that if we showed someone what life could be like, there might be an epiphany moment, a moment of transformation, for the individual. I knew of a residential rehab not far from Burnley, and so I bypassed all normal procedure, and I just rang them. I asked if I could bring Mark to have a look at the centre just so he could see what might be possible for him. Surprisingly, the rehab agreed.

'Mark, you told me one time that ye wanted to get clean and not just be surviving, d'ye remember?' I said to Mark the following Saturday.

'That's right, I did,' replied my friend. He was very wobbly on his feet that day so again we were sitting on the wall outside the church, watching the world go by together sipping a brew each.

'Well, will ye come to the rehab if I drive you there?'

Mark hesitated for a moment, then he nodded.

'I will. You just tell me where I have to be and when and I'll be there.'

We agreed the date and time, and naturally I thought Mark wouldn't show up. I asked him to come to me to prove he was willing and wanting to go, and I would drive us there. Amazingly, Mark showed up on time and looking like he'd made an effort with his appearance. Obviously, he still looked ragged because he is a man who lives hour to hour, day to day financially, and that is reflected in what he wears, but his hair was smoothed down and his hands were clean, and even those small changes filled me with a quiet kind of happiness. He got into the passenger seat carrying a can of 9 per cent and off we went.

'What if they won't let me in?' He was becoming increasingly anxious as we travelled out of the town centre.

'You're just having a look round today, Mark. Try and enjoy our little trip and take it as a little bit of inspiration, perhaps,' I suggested as we pulled into the car park.

'Welcome,' said one of the guys who was staying at the rehab, as we walked in. 'I'm Tony and I'm here to show yous around.' He had a thick Geordie accent and a big grin.

'Thank you, that's brilliant,' I replied, trying not to feel as much excitement about today as I did. I didn't want to set Mark – or myself – up for disappointment, and I fervently hoped I'd done the right thing though it was an unorthodox move.

Tony gave us a guided tour, and I literally saw Mark's face light up as we sat with some of the clients and they talked about where they'd come from. They had mostly been in the same sort of circumstances as my friend; problems of homelessness, family abuse, neglect and addiction ran rife. Mark sat and listened to it all, his face a picture of wonder.

'I'm in a bad way. I'm a mess,' Mark kept saying. He was shaking and his limp seemed, if anything, to have got worse.

'I was the same when I got in here,' said Tony. 'That was a year ago, mate, just a year. It's amazin' what can happen in a few months in a place like this, eh.'

Another guy spoke up at this point: 'I'm nine months clean, mate, and if I can do it, anyone can,' and with that he gave a throaty laugh.

Mark looked gobsmacked. I could see that if someone had said to him, 'Go on, lad, you can have a place here right now,' he would've jumped at the chance.

Sadly, that wasn't why we were here.

When it was time to leave, we thanked the guys and Tony for the tour and for their honesty.

'Can I come here? Can I come here?' Mark kept saying as we said our goodbyes. It was everything Mark had needed to see and hear, but there was one major problem: he had to be off alcohol before he was able to be considered for rehabilitation. How that was going to happen was anyone's guess.

Mark was euphoric as he stepped back into my car, and it

was really sad to then have to drop him back to those awful chalets where he said he was being bullied and robbed.

As we approached this place, Mark said: 'Turn left here, Father Alex, and ye can drop me off.'

My heart sank when I saw it was right outside an offie, an off-licence.

'Er, ye don't have three quid for a can, do ye?' he asked, sheepishly.

'Sorry, Mark, I don't,' I replied.

'Alright, see ye then, Father.'

'See ye, Mark,' I said sadly. I don't know what I was expecting, but I still hoped that somewhere underneath all the damage was a spark of hope for what might be.

I discovered Mark needed to attend a local treatment centre to begin cutting down, and this, if successful, would pave the way to entering the rehabilitation process. Mark had been attending for a few weeks, and my optimism started to come back; that is, until I received a phone call.

Sarah shouted from the hallway: 'Alex, are ye there? Phone call for you ...'

'Hello, is that Father Alex?'

'Yes it is. How can I help?' I replied.

'This is Inspire, the treatment centre Mark should've been attending. We haven't seen him for a while and wondered if ye knew if he was okay?'

Not for the first time, I sighed.

'I haven't seen him for a couple of weeks meself, and I was beginning to wonder too. Let me have a drive round the parish and see if I can find him,' I said.

I got into my car and went off, going to Mark's usual haunts to see if anyone knew where he was. Finally, I found him, apparently asleep on a discarded sofa near to his previous accommodation.

'What's to do, Mark? How are ye? We've been worried about ye. You haven't been goin' to your meetings ...'

Mark roused himself a little. He wasn't asleep but he wasn't in great shape either.

'Sorry, Father, I forgot, like ...' he muttered, trying to turn over.

'What's goin' on here, Mark? Are ye sleeping here now or what?' I asked, not sure I wanted to know the answer. My friend looked unwell to say the least. His face was puffy and grey and his clothes were filthy.

'It's alright. I've got accommodation so I don't just kip down here. Someone gave me a sleepin' bag and I've got my 9 per cent. It could be worse ...'

'I'm not sure it could, if I'm honest, Mark. Ye can't get a place in that rehab without attending your meetings.'

'I know, I'll go back, Father, I promise ...' Mark grumbled, closing his eyes again.

I realise there are no guarantees with someone as sick with addiction as Mark. It is my hope that my friend keeps moving forward, and might one day experience what a life of sobriety could bring him. There would be few things in my ministry that would give me greater joy than seeing Mark recover and be well. I live for the day that we will go and do something together in celebration of his recovery. He is somebody who through his own self-combustion has effectively been written off. It was his decision not to register with a GP or seek help, but, until now, nobody has ever really worried about him or really wanted that change for him. If he died, it wouldn't block many people's landscape, and harsher people might say that it would be him getting what he deserved, that there would be one less person for tax-payers to worry about.

If that is somebody's view of someone with the level of unresolved trauma and chaos that my friend lives with, then it's a sad reflection on the society we live in, and yet I know that for Mark it could go either way. I'm not naïve. I know he has to put the hard yards in. At the rehab, I kept saying to him: 'That could be you, mate. That could be you …' Mark's struggles continue. He turns up for 10am appointments at the drug and alcohol service he is meant to be attending in order to be given a place in rehab at 3pm, though he has let me register him with a GP who carried out some basic physical and mental health checks. With the lowest score for both being 40 points, it wasn't exactly a moment of celebration when he scored 40 on one and 39 on the other, but as they say, when you hit rock bottom, the only way is up.

I came up with the idea of interviewing local people about their faith as a way of entertaining people stuck inside their homes during the lockdowns, little knowing how it would progress. These podcasts are called 'The God Cast', and some famous names have been kind enough to talk to me about Christianity, their faith and their lives both in the spotlight and outside of it. Celebrities and politicians such as Eamonn Holmes, Alastair Campbell, Edwina Currie, Lou Macari and many others.

'So what d'ye think, Mum?' I said after making my mother listen to one of the broadcasts.

She looked at me, and though she was born a southerner she has absorbed the northern way of saying it as it occurs to her, however mildly offensive or rude.

'Well, Alex, I must say ye look a lot better in your photo on the website than ye do in real life …'

I almost choked on my digestive.

'That's a bit rude, Mum,' I laughed.

'Oh well, ye know it's best to tell the truth. Just like when ye met Sarah. She was far too attractive for you but ye did well there, didn't ye?'

This conversation, such as it was, was veering off the subject rapidly.

'But what did ye think of the podcast?' I asked again. Mum, though, was by now bustling off to the kitchen to wash up her cup and get off to bingo.

We'd been listening to Mark, who was a guest later on as the podcast evolved. It is always wonderful to listen to a famous person talking about their lives, but I wanted normal people, the people of my community, to have a voice too, so I'd asked Mark if he wanted to talk about the trials and tribulations he'd faced through his life, hoping it might be cathartic.

'So, what's your goal in life, Mark?'

'I just want to exist,' he replied.

'Do ye ever think you'll get clean?'

'If I did, I think it'd kill me,' he answered. He'd been very upfront about his life, both in the podcast and in other discussions we'd had over the months. I find it hard to believe that a human being can ever be content with just existing, and I wanted to help him to develop aspirations that went beyond this.

'I can survive in this life. It's like I know the rules, I know what to do to get by,' he tried to explain to me.

This fascinated me, because to an outsider like myself he didn't look like he was surviving very well at all. He didn't seem to care what anyone else thought of him, his appearance or lifestyle, and I had to respect that in some ways.

Mark talked about his childhood and his early years on the podcast, and again we've spoken in more depth about it since. I think in every conversation I have with him, I'm looking for that chink of light, the place where the seed of transformation might burst into life.

'Mark's not a famous face, he's not somebody you will know, but he's become a friend of mine. Over the last year, he's been using the foodbank and coming to Breakfast Club. Mark, you're a Burnley lad, yeah?'

'Yes, I'm Burnley through and through. I grew up in Cliviger, then we moved close to Turf Moor [the Burnley FC football ground], and that were my family home for many years,' Mark said.

'So, what was life like growing up in Cliviger, Mark? What was that like?'

'Beautiful. We left there when I was six years old and moved to Burnley,' Mark continued, his eye blackened and bruised from yet another fight at his accommodation.

'Were ye a big family?'

'No, we were a really small family; me mum, me dad and me sister,' he replied.

'And schooldays, what were schooldays like for you? Were they okay, or troubled?'

'Quite troubled,' Mark said, which was no surprise I'm sure. So much addiction and trauma seems to be rooted in the past.

Cliviger is an affluent area of Burnley originally, and is a really beautiful area of the town. Mark told me he used to help the local farmers make hay, and in some ways it sounded idyllic. This didn't seem to last long, though. By the time he was twelve or thirteen years old, he'd got in with the wrong crowd and started sniffing glue, saying he had to have friends and had to survive. The family of the girl he was seeing ran a hardware store where glue was readily available. The pathway into addiction seemed inevitable – and it makes me worry about some of the other people I see day to day, as there are so many who seem to be going down that same route. From what I have seen with Mark, it's extremely difficult to get back onto a good path once that road has been taken. He has spoken about the glue sniffing leading to smoking cannabis, and then, again inevitably it seems, to dealing cannabis. He even boasted that he grew the best cannabis in Burnley.

I wonder if Mark, and all those like him with the same problems, knew they were heading down a one-way road to destruction?

'Did ye know you were headin' down the wrong path?' I'd asked him.

Mark sniffed and his face looked momentarily sad.

'Yes, I knew.'

'So, why did you go down it? What was the reason?' I wanted to understand how it is that people descend into the horrors they experience.

'Er, maybe it was lack of education, and lack of intelligence even. I'm not a thick person, me. I've got the T-shirts, layer after layer of T-shirts, but now I'm an alcoholic.'

Mark is someone who knew the road was full of No Entry signs and yet he couldn't stop himself going down them. What astounded me about him is that he attributed this to a lack of intelligence, but I didn't see that at all. The way I understand it was that Mark was following the wrong damn road map! There seems to have been no one to guide or advise him at key points in his life; as a teenager, then as a young man.

Apparently, Mark was earning good money dealing cannabis. It was quite lucrative, though it wasn't going to buy him his yacht in the South of France. At the same time, he became part of a notorious football hooliganism gang called The Suicide Squad, and he appears to have enjoyed engaging with narcotics and violence as well. Naturally, that progressed into shooting up heroin and he started dealing that too, though there was never any money in it for him. Anything he earned, he used to spend on taking heroin, and he was never one of the 'big boys'. Eventually, he was caught with a huge amount of heroin in his possession, about two and a half kilos of it, which was worth a lot of money. He told me he was stopped by armed police who held guns in his face and dragged him to the ground. He has always said he was never the money man, but in that world you don't grass people up so he took responsibility for the hoard. He was sentenced to four years in prison, and the local newspaper covered the court case, describing him as 'Burnley's King Pin' drug dealer. I got the feeling he quite liked the accolade, but the reality was that he was far from that.

It was really strange talking to Mark about prison, because when he did speak about it, it sounded like it was a period of his life when he was quite settled. There was a structure to his days, with regular decent meals and regular sleep. Before prison he had been a prolific shoplifter to buy glue, then drugs, but while behind bars he was given valium and methadone twice a day by the chemist. Sadly, prison also introduced him to the deadly drug Spice, and by the time he was released he was also addicted to valium, methadone and temazepam. He said something that really struck me. He said that alcohol was 'the worst drug of all because it's available twenty-four hours a day, seven days a week'. There was a logic to that statement that summed up how pervasive and potentially damaging our relationship to alcohol really is as a society.

Mark worked briefly as a sous-chef in a good hotel in Cornwall, but couldn't stay off the drink and so left and returned here. He told me he's tried to get sober many times, but somehow always crashes back onto the booze. He set himself a rule that he couldn't drink nine per cent before 6pm, trying to control his addiction, but soon that became 5pm, then 4pm, then 3pm, then 12pm, then, before he knew it, he was reaching for a can the minute he woke up in the morning. It was heartbreaking to hear. There is so much waste of potential, of a life that could've been lived well.

A year after being ordained as a deacon I was priested, which meant I was ordained for a second time, this time by the bishop at the same cathedral but surrounded by my peers. I'd spent my year helping out where I could. I was privileged to help out in the classroom of the church school in my parish. I was there to help them read, and to help with Year Three maths. The kids were great, but I soon discovered my level of attainment was well below the levels of the seven- and eight-year-olds I was 'helping'. With older parishioners, I was also given the honour of being the gravy monitor at a pensioners' community group. When, after a year, I was finally ordained into the priesthood, it felt like the culmination of years of trying, waiting and learning.

The priests that surrounded me, which included Reverend Richard, also laid their hands on me, touching my shoulders as the sacred words were said. The laying on of hands is a beautiful symbolic gesture, inviting the Holy Spirit to descend upon a priest. It is the special part of the ceremony, the transformational part. We were standing in a horseshoe and I remember looking into one of the other priests' eyes and there was a real sense that we'd done it, we'd made it to priesthood. I don't say that the Holy Spirit descended upon me at the moment of my transformation, but it felt like an affirmation, as though the Holy Spirit was with me throughout. I felt God had been there all through the difficulties. I saw that I had wanted to become ordained at my pace, and God was showing me that my time would come at his pace. If things are to happen, they happen when God decides. Being priested felt like a doff in my cap to my resilience. I learnt so much about my character. I will never give up on anything now. If I hadn't kept going, I wouldn't be a priest now. If I hadn't kept going, I wouldn't be able to help people now. Whenever anyone comes to me and they're going through difficulties, I tell them to keep going. Always just keep going. I say that to Mark a lot, though I worry about him all the time. If nothing else, I can encourage resilience in those who come to me. I also hope I have become a more patient person because of the difficulties, a more empathetic minister.

From then onwards, I was able to bless objects and people, and celebrate the sacrament of Holy Communion, which I never tire of. The beauty of it never dissipates with repetition. The poetry of the liturgy, The Prayer of Humble Access, moves me every time. It says: 'We do not presume to come to this your table, O merciful Lord, trusting in our own righteousness, but in your abundant and great mercies.' It talks of God's love and mercy for us, and says that we are fed by him so that he may live within us, and us within him. It is beautiful. It is said just before the bread and wine undergoes that symbolic or literal transformation (depending upon your beliefs) of transformation, or transubstantiation as it is properly called. Where bread becomes flesh, where wine becomes blood. An extraordinary symbol of change. This prayer transforms my mind and my mood. Even if I wake up feeling shite, the sacrament always restores me.

It pains me that I cannot restore Mark, or the many others who come to me and tell me of their addictions and struggles. It pains me that I cannot change the direction of their lives, though it never stops me trying.

13.

INJUSTICE

'... a time to be silent, and a time to speak ...'

Ecclesiastes 3:7, 'A Time for Everything'

'So, how long did ye have to wait for that buggy, Jenny?' I asked as I dunked yet another custard cream into my tea at the anxiety group.

The restrictions had eased and life was returning to normal, so the groups I was privileged to go to were back up and running. It was great to see Jenny. She looked just the same with her short hair, leggings, trainers and hoodie.

'Fuckin' twenty weeks, give or take,' Jenny Swears-a-Lot replied, eyebrows raised, looking round the room as if anyone would dare to question her.

'Twenty weeks. If I wasn't a priest, I'd swear right now,' I said, crossly. 'They made ye wait that long before ye could get help with your profoundly autistic son who has special needs and hurts himself because he can't see the edges of pavements and kerbs ...' I felt bloody furious.

'Yeah,' Jenny said, shrugging. 'What are ye goin' to do? I

had no choice but to wait. They kept tellin' me there were delays and problems with supplies, but anyway, we've got it now.'

'I'm glad to hear it,' I said, feeling anything but. It was a scandal, making a young mum with five kids wait for 20 weeks. It felt unfair. More than that, it felt unjust.

At this point, the group fell silent. What could we say? Jenny's life seemed to be a never-ending series of crappy situations.

The people I mention in this book have allowed me to share their stories, something that leaves me feeling deeply humbled. More importantly perhaps is the fact they've allowed me into their worlds. Their worlds are beset by a tsunami of problems that are affecting the whole of our nation: mental health problems, poverty, the debt crisis, loan sharks, an unfair benefits system that keeps people waiting for weeks before pay-outs, mothers choosing between paying for gas to heat their homes or food to feed their children, injustices in the workplace, zero hours contracts, high rents, deprivation and hopelessness, to name just a few. I know people who shouldn't be alive, they really shouldn't, and it constantly amazes me how the will to live keeps people going.

The scars left by the pandemic, including long NHS waiting lists, may never heal in my community. The wounds being inflicted by the rising cost of living may scar my community for years to come. Yet, on top of these already-challenging circumstances, I come across people dealing with things that still have the capacity to shock me, and perhaps this is where Ecclesiastes tells us there is a time for speaking out. As much as what Jenny deals with shocks me, there has been an even bigger test of my faith involving the death of a local girl called Kelsey Devlin.

This story feels like the culmination of much of the injustice experienced in the lives of the people around me as they struggle to be heard, as they feel forgotten about or marginalised. It is a natural progression, if you like, from the lives I've shared of families with no furniture and people who turn up at church skint, begging for food and money. There were very few things that surprised me in the retail world by the time my career ended there, but a lot of what I see in my ministry shocks me, and none more so than meeting the Devlin family.

Burnley has a community culture, maybe because it's a small town and not a city. As I have said, it is almost as if any injustice is felt by the whole community together. If somebody is hurt, we're all hurt. If one person dies, we all mourn, and maybe that's unique to the estate setting. Everybody knows each other. Everybody knows each other's business and, therefore, identifies with each other's troubles. I knew of the Devlin family as I'd seen Judy and her husband Sean, and their many children, at events, but I didn't know them much beyond that. One day that all changed.

'Hello, Father Alex?' the female voice said on the telephone.

'Yes, it's Father Alex speaking. How can I help?' I was flicking through some emails at the time, and was guilty of being a bit distracted.

'If you wouldn't mind, my husband Sean and I would like you to come over and talk about doing a memorial service for our daughter who passed away recently. Is that something you could do?' At this point, her voice went quiet.

'Is that Judy?' I said, recognising her voice. All thoughts of the emails had vanished.

'Yes it is. Sorry, I should've said.'

'That's alright. I'm sorry to hear of your loss; of course I'll pop by. Is this afternoon okay?'

I already knew where Judy and Sean lived because Reverend Kat knew them quite well and had been to visit a few times.

'I'll be back for dinner,' I shouted to Sarah who had just got in.

'Okay Alex, hope it goes well,' Sarah replied as I shut the door behind me.

At this stage, I thought I was just going to have to say a few words over a dodgy microphone and portable amplifier on the rec, and so I went around to their house thinking I'd be there for half an hour, while trying to say the right things, share condolences with the family, make plans for the service and head home.

I couldn't have been more wrong.

Kelsey's family lives in one of the most deprived neighbourhoods in Burnley, on the edge of the Stoops area, which was a sprawling estate where many of my parishioners lived. I knew it well by now so I headed to their street in the summer sunshine. The usual enormous barking dogs baring their teeth and snarling greeted me as I walked. I dodged the usual graffiti, dog shit and rubbish, trying to think what I might know about this family. I knew Judy and Jenny were mates, and I'd seen Judy at various community events. I knew the family were the absolute heart of their community, and so I knew this death would have wide-ranging significance to the area as a whole.

Judy opened the door of the four-bed terraced house they rented privately. Her blonde hair looked shiny and she was wearing a pretty necklace and a nice black dress. She looked exhausted, though. There were shadows under her eyes and, immediately, I could see she was grieving deeply.

'Hello, Judy. Thank you for inviting me to come and see ye, though I'm extremely sorry for your loss. You said your daughter had passed away? I'm so sorry to hear this,' I started, but Sean interrupted me almost straight away as if his emotions had been pent up and were now bursting out of him.

'Our Kelsey, our eldest is dead. We don't know how she died. We don't know where she's buried. All we know is she went to Pakistan a healthy young woman and then a few weeks later she was gone and no one can tell us where she is or where our grandchildren are.'

There was a pause as we all digested what Sean, a lean-looking man in his late fifties or early sixties, was saying. His face was twisted with anger and emotion, and I just looked between them both, completely unsure what to say next.

'I'm sorry, I don't know what happened to Kelsey, so ye might want to tell me about her and what ye think went on,' I suggested.

Various young people and children milled about as we talked with a sort of revolving-door quality; when one would come in, another might go out, and this just kept going on and on. There was a frantic air in the house, which wasn't huge despite the number of people that lived in it. There were toys strewn everywhere amid the clean but basic furniture. The house wasn't a palace but it was a lived-in family home and it was obvious Judy took pride in it.

Judy placed a hand on her husband's knee in an attempt to calm him. There was something so loving, so kind in that gesture that I saw instantly how she must be holding not just herself, but the whole family together. She picked up a photo and there was a young woman's smiling face on it. She was beautiful with shining dark hair and beautiful big brown eyes that had the same twinkle in them as her mother's, though Judy's were dulled by sadness.

'This is Kelsey. The photo was taken shortly before she took her kids, our grandkids Zara and Zain, to Islamabad to see her ex's mother as, apparently, she was very ill. We don't know much more than that. Zara is eight and Zain is six, and we haven't seen them since. They're still in Pakistan and it's been weeks since they told us Kelsey had died. Our daughter was only twenty-seven years old. She was the eldest of our family, and we're just in shock. We can't believe she's gone, Father Alex ...'

Judy wiped her eyes with a tissue while Sean fought back tears. I sat opposite them in their lounge, almost unable to comprehend what they'd been telling me. I handed Judy back the photo and she placed it on her lap, holding it with both hands as if she might never let it go.

'She'd been in Islamabad just the three weeks when they said she was in hospital with Covid. Then they changed their story and said she had a stroke and sepsis. We couldn't make head nor tail of it,' said Sean.

'Who told ye all this?' I said, incredulously. I'd never heard anything like it in my life.

'I think it was a family relative over there, but I'm not sure. They rang us out of the blue. We asked the Foreign Office to go and send someone to the hospital, which was in

Rawalpindi,' Judy added. By now, several of the older children, teenagers, were perched on the settee arms and sitting cross-legged on the floor. They all looked exactly how they must be feeling – shocked and utterly distraught.

'No one went. Or if they did, they weren't allowed in. We're not really sure. We didn't even know she'd died until after they'd buried her …' Sean broke down at this point, and one of his daughters put her arms around him. It was obvious this was an intensely loving family, and they all shared the same pain equally.

'This is the death certificate. It contradicts again what we were told. It says our Kelsey died of sepsis, a stroke and cardio-pulmonary arrest, and they've put her age wrong, and said she was a Muslim, which she wasn't. It also says she was married and had epilepsy! All this is just totally untrue!' Judy carried on the story.

'Sorry, how come she'd been allowed to travel given that the Covid bans are still in place?' I asked.

'They gave her special permission because of the grandmother. I'm sure Kelsey said they'd told her she was dying or somethin' and she wanted to see the grandkids for the last time,' Sean said in a muffled voice.

'It's all still a mystery, and we don't know who to turn to. I rang the British Embassy in Islamabad asking them to check on my daughter, but to my knowledge they didn't do that.'

'Sean also rang Lancashire Police and told them, but they said it was out of their jurisdiction and we should speak to the Foreign Office or the Home Office, only we'd already tried that. We want answers, Father Alex,' Judy finished.

'I can see that. I would feel exactly the same. It's a deeply unpalatable situation. I can't express how sorry I feel for you all, and I'll help in any way I can. But didn't you want to talk about a memorial as well?' I wasn't sure where to begin with helping them, but I could help them sort out some kind of Christian remembrance.

'Actually, I don't know, Father. We're hopin' the Foreign Office might get involved and bring her body home. We've asked them to repatriate her, bring her home to us so we can give her a proper funeral,' said Judy, and the look on her face was agonising. Without a body, they couldn't move forward with their lives and grieve properly. They couldn't grieve properly because they desperately wanted Kelsey home. Their predicament was pure tragedy.

There is a time to be silent and that is when the family are relating their hurt and their loss. It is a time to listen and reflect. But as the verse says, there is a time to speak out, and I knew then that I would be the one to do it for them. These were working-class people who lived on the bread line. In the eyes of society, they were unimportant. I could see that, and yet these were well-loved members of our community, people who were at the coalface of hardship and who contributed so much to many lives. I had to help them.

I didn't return home until late that evening.

'Your dinner's in the oven. What happened, Alex?' Sarah said, looking at me with her wonderful, gentle gaze. I still pinch myself when I look at her and realise she became my wife. My wife Sarah and my family have always been my towers of strength, and so I took all this to her. Even now, over thirty years into our life together, I look at her and cannot believe I was lucky enough to marry her. Mum was right. She's too good for me. That night, she sat and listened as I wept and railed against an uncaring system that saw good people like the Devlins left to cope with an uncopeable situation entirely unsupported by the powers-that-be.

'I've got to help them, Sarah. They have so many questions they feel have been unanswered.'

The next day, I went back round to the Devlins' home. I rang the Lancashire Police and was informed that nothing could be done because it was an international matter. I then tried to get through to the Foreign Office in Islamabad, but was unable to speak to anyone. I spoke to the Home Office in London on that Saturday afternoon, saying 'Could somebody please just help the family get answers?' I was told this was a police matter and to go back to Lancashire Police and they should appoint an international liaison officer who could pursue the matter on their behalf. The individual I spoke to also told me that if it was someone more high profile, then something would be being done about it. I rang 101 and spoke to Lancashire Police again, as if this was somehow less serious than a 999 call. I was told we needed to be referred to a sergeant. I asked for a log number and wasn't given one, instead I was told somebody would get back to me. I stayed at the Devlin home for two and a half hours, just making calls, trying to get someone to recognise that this family had lost a healthy, strong young woman in unusual circumstances and they wanted, no they deserved, to have answers. It amazed me that nobody had rung them from the Foreign Office. No one had rung from the Home Office either to ask how they were. No one had rung them from the police – even just to check in on the family and say sorry for their loss abroad.

If this had happened in the UK, the family would surely have been appointed a police liaison officer. Meanwhile,

Lancashire Police weren't particularly helpful, and I was told there was nothing they could do so I suggested it might have been good practice to take a statement from the family, who believed there were suspicious circumstances to the death. This prompted a visit by Lancashire police officers to the family home. The conversation was quite raucous as, by then, I was surrounded by Kelsey's large extended family and friends who were vociferous in their opinions. It wasn't for me to speak on their behalf, so that day I was just there for moral – and spiritual – support. I said nothing and, instead, listened to a bereaved family express their grief.

It was clear the family didn't feel they had been given the truth about Kelsey's death, and they made that very clear to the two police officers who came to take Sean's statement.

The *Guardian* newspaper even got wind of the story and journalist Helen Pidd came to interview them all, while her colleague journalist Shah Meer Baloch reported in Islamabad. They ran a story, but to me the real injustice was that, until others such as myself and the reporters got involved, the family had made little headway in their quest for answers. Once the press shone a light on the family's tragedy, there was finally some traction. According to the article, our local MP requested Kelsey's body be exhumed and returned to the UK so a full autopsy could take place to establish once and for all the manner of her passing. Sean and Judy wanted transparency. They wanted to be sure that what they'd been told was, in fact, true. They wanted closure so they could mourn their daughter with the dignity they felt had been denied them. The MP Mr Higginbotham also asked for the grandchildren to be returned home. To this day, the family has not seen those two children. They never came home.

'We don't know if we'll ever see Zara and Zain again,' Judy said bleakly one afternoon. I'd invited her along to St Matthew's to talk about the memorial idea. It was a few months after we'd made that initial contact and the conversation had changed from a memorial to considering how we could have a funeral for Kelsey despite there being no body.

'Sean won't ever stop askin' for her to come home, but I think we have to find a way to move our lives on, and I think perhaps holding a funeral for Kesley might be the right way. I want her to have a proper Christian service, and I want to celebrate her life with all our family and the estate,' she added.

We were sitting in two of the seats about mid-way down the aisle. The sun was streaming in through the glass windows high up in the vaulted ceilings, and Doris was somewhere, cleaning something, because we could hear the intermittent screech of our well-used vacuum cleaner echoing through the church building.

'I don't think my daughter will ever be comin' home,' Judy said, gazing down to the altar.

'Would you like us to say a prayer for her?' I asked.

Judy smiled. Her eyes were glazed with tears.

'God, hear our prayer. Please watch over the Devlin family, bring peace where there has been little, bring solace and comfort where there has been none, and watch over Kelsey wherever she may be,' I prayed quietly.

We stayed like that, hands together in the universal sign of prayer, eyes shut, for a few minutes, soaking in the serenity of that brief moment.

The family was entirely without the funds to travel to Pakistan to try and find out where their daughter's remains were buried. I was told several times that the cost of repatriation would be too high, and it simply wasn't going to happen. I couldn't help but wonder if this would be the same story for someone famous or well connected. Sean asked me to report the death as suspicious to the Islamabad authorities. It felt like a last-ditch attempt at uncovering the answers they longed for, and so I agreed.

'Fuck's sake!' I swore loudly at the computer.

'You okay, Alex?' Sarah poked her head around my office door.

'Not really,' I replied. 'It won't let me download the form I need to fill in to report Kelsey's death to the Pakistani officials because it's corrupted!'

Sarah looked at me.

'Come to bed, it's late, Alex. Try again in the morning; you're just one man and ye can't fix it tonight.'

I knew she was right, but I just couldn't leave it. I felt a responsibility to this family who had already, in a short few months, come to mean so much to me.

'I'll be up in a bit,' I said, returning to the screen.

'Fuck's sake,' I muttered under my breath. There was one small glimmer of hope. I'd rung the Home Office again, and this time one of the staff had said they'd raise the issue with the Islamabad authorities on their behalf.

I felt deeply connected to this family, and still do. Like many of the people I have the privilege of serving, they are voiceless. They are underprivileged, marginalised and unimportant to the authorities both here and in Pakistan. Yet they are part of the lifeblood of this community. They have problems of financial insecurity and now they have the grief of losing their beautiful daughter. Sean and Judy have gone from being loving parents and grandparents to grieving them all.

Putting everything to one side, this is a family already living in challenging circumstances. They are beautifully working class, very down-to-earth. They live on a low income. They are in a very difficult position, yet they are a deeply loving family, a family I think the world of, and I will do everything I can to help them. Again, I cannot help but ask whether this role should fall to a vicar. It is not my job to guide a family through international difficulties and legal issues, yet I will be by their side all the way. It is not my job to ensure that police statements are made, leads are followed, and a family's voice and feelings are heard, yet I will be there offering whatever support I can. But I also ask, who else will do this for them? Who else is really listening to them? As far as I can see, I've been the only service to offer bereavement support, counselling and financial assistance.

This is a complicated matter and it does have potential legal implications, yet surely they should have more support than one person who is untrained in this field can offer? The family does have a social worker, but I cannot see any empathy within the services that offer statutory support. In the wider world, I cannot see compassion within the legal or the international framework. It is my contention that no one cares because they are poor, because they are working class, and so they are abandoned. I often forget that it works that way. Because I am living and working with the Devlins, and all my parishioners, I forget they are labelled 'poor', I forget they are labelled 'marginalised'. All I see are people trying to do their best, who are real flesh-and-blood people with hearts and souls. I don't look at them and judge them as poor; I look and think, 'How can I help?'

It doesn't cost anything to do that, to think like that, and that's what pisses me off. People who are poor continue to be poor. In the time since Kelsey's death nothing has got better for the family, nothing has been resolved. I challenge my wife Sarah to imagine how we would feel if our healthy daughter went abroad and died suddenly. How would we feel if we never saw her again? How would we feel not knowing the exact circumstances around her death, and not knowing where her body was buried, and if all of that had happened before we were even told? It's a fucking disgrace. This should not be allowed to happen in today's world – and yet it does happen, it keeps on happening. The Devlins were having to fight for answers at a time when they were grieving, when they are already battling for survival.

I hope what I'm saying here pisses people off. I hope I'm stirring up a hornet's nest because something needs to be done. I don't care about any of the reasons and excuses we've been given for the lack of action, because all I know is that a family in their moment of crisis were forgotten about. I saw their suffering every day, every week, at not being able to afford to fly out to find their daughter's grave and put flowers there. I keep returning to the question, 'Why has this been allowed to happen?' Who's to say this won't be happening to other families? A senior person whom I cannot name said to me in one of the many phone calls I have made over the months: 'You'll not get the answers, and you'll make yourself ill trying. You can't leave it, can you?' Well, I couldn't leave it – and I still can't leave it. These questions remain unanswered today.

What actually happened to Kelsey Devlin?

Why can't she come home for a Christian burial?

Why can't the Devlins see their grandchildren?

These are uncomfortable questions, and I don't know the answers, and I'll go to my grave with that.

'Judy, I don't know how Kelsey died. I have no idea whether what you've been told is the truth or not, and I'm not qualified to tell ye. I do know that I promise I'll be a voice for you, as long as you want me to be. I'll be by your side however long you want me to be.' That was my vow to this lady in the church that day.

We didn't say much. We sat together in companionable silence, then she talked and I listened, and a plan started to crystallise.

Ecclesiastes 3:1–8, 'A Time for Everything', is an extraordinarily beautiful passage that reminds us about there being a right time to mourn, a right time to go within, and a right time to come out and speak. It reminds us that God has given us time enough for everything that needs to be completed in this life – and I have to believe that is true for the Devlins. They deserve that at least. Kelsey deserves that at least.

14.

KELSEY

'The Lord gave, and the Lord hath taken away ...'

Job 1:21

The young girls in the seats at the front of the church wiped tears from their eyes, where a minute ago they'd been chewing gum and nattering.

'I can see lots of tears, and I feel very emotional, so if ye want to cry then cry. We've come here today to remember and celebrate Kelsey. To give thanks for her life. To remember what she means and has meant to every single one of you here this afternoon,' I said as the congregation hushed.

'I'm so sorry that we're here. I'm so grateful that Sean and Judy have allowed me into their world, and I understand the terrible and difficult circumstances of Kelsey's passing. But today, we're here to remember the good things she brought to us just by being around.

'Let us pray ...'

Kelsey's funeral was the hardest thing I've done in my ministry. Trying to explain a death that was unexplainable, trying to comfort a family that wasn't just grieving but felt angry as well, was the most challenging and painful experience of my priesthood – both for my own faith and emotional wellbeing and for theirs. This was a family with no body to grieve over. The Lord truly had taken away, and none of us could make any sense of it.

'Father Alex, we've decided we definitely want a proper Christian funeral service for Kelsey. She deserves that ...' Judy had smiled her usual warm, loving smile, as she spoke to me.

She'd popped into Fun Church with her son Declan, and year-old grandchild, and while kids were singing nursery rhymes with Reverend Kat and Julie, we had a moment to speak. It was a crisp early autumn day and we both still had our coats on as we sat together.

'Okay, Judy. I need to think very hard about how to do it, but we'll find a way,' I said, smiling back though I knew that planning a funeral without a body might be a difficult process.

'Judy, sorry to mention this, but the practicalities mean there'll be no coffin for Kelsey, no focus for everyone as they look towards the altar. What we could do is have a screen with a projector, and we could record people's memories and tributes, and you might want to have some flowers or something at the front so people have a focus. What d'ye reckon?'

'I'll have to speak to me husband, but it sounds alright, Father. I know he is ready to do the service now. I think even he sees we won't ever have her body back ...' Judy replied.

'And any news about Zara and Zain?' I said, as a shaft of sunlight streamed through the church.

As we both watched dust motes whirl and spin, she shook her head.

'No news, but we'll never stop tryin' to get them home. If I thought I'd never see them again ...'

Neither of us spoke.

'It's decided then,' I said, gruffly. 'I'll speak to Reverend Kat and we'll create a service just for Kelsey.'

That service was now underway. The church was packed to the rafters as we knew it would be. Looking out over that sea of faces as I stepped back from my welcome speech, and with Kat stepping forward to read a passage from the Bible, I felt emotional but also uplifted at the sight of all that love, all that community, all those people who cared. Caring is our most valuable commodity. In a strange and changing world, kindness and love is worth everything. At times, such as for these people in my congregation now, it might be the only thing they have. They hurt together. They mourn together. They have each other. In some ways, they are the most blessed among us. Perhaps that is what Jesus meant when he said those words, 'Blessed are the poor', because they have each other in ways that most of us with our nice lives cannot fathom.

The wonderful volunteers at the church, along with Reverend Kat and myself, had set up everything as we normally would, with that one main exception: the space reserved for the coffin was empty. I wanted to fill that space with prayer. We lit all the candles and made the church as beautiful as we could. We set up the screen and projector so that family and friends could share photos, memories and stories of this young woman who was buried somewhere in Pakistan, far away from her loved ones.

Reverend Kat read a description of heaven from Revelation 21:4. It says: 'God will wipe away every tear from their eye, and there will be no more death, no more sadness, for the old order of things has passed away.' This is Jesus' promise, to comfort and wipe away sorrow and tears. It is his promise to end all pain, all suffering. I pray that is true for the Devlin family, because it would be hard to express on these pages the level of suffering experienced by Sean and Judy, and their family. They were in torment – and it continues to this day.

There would usually be a lit candle beside the coffin, or one would be carried into the church in front of the procession, and so, instead, we had candles on the church's beautiful carved wooden candelabras at the front of the church. The family had ordered a large floral-style tribute, with Kelsey's name spelt out in green and white, and this was sitting on the floor slap-bang at the front of the aisle so no one could miss seeing it. It was perfect. I read out memories written by family and friends.

'I'll always remember the times she came to her mum's with a McDonald's. She loved her food and she ate it that quick. She was lookin' for her bank card as she'd lost it, and I said, "You've probably eaten it."'

'When grandma sent us to the chippie for chips and a curry, she went in and I started shining a laser in the eyes and the next thing, they chased us with a knife all the way across town on our scooter. We crossed a field. The scooter lost a wheel and she face-planted on the grass. Chips went all over. Let's say grandma wasn't pleased with her chips. She said, "You two can't be trusted even goin' for chips without gettin' into trouble."'

'I just remember takin' her to football matches as a young girl. At the end of the match I'd have to get the team to give me a push to get the van goin'. Kelsey always told me to get the van fixed and to stop showin' her up.'

I could've gone on and on recounting anecdotes and treasured memories, there were so many. The congregation were laughing and smiling, nodding their heads as they remembered her antics. I felt like I knew her character a little by now, and she seemed lots of fun.

'I'll never forget the time Kelsey forgot we had moved house. She climbed through our old house to use the toilet. She then came to our new house laughin, sayin' she'd climbed in the window to have a wee and forgot we'd moved!'

That made people chuckle, but the last messages were distinctly different, and brought us back to reality with a bump.

'Since you were suddenly taken away, the hardest thing to cope with is not knowing why. There are questions left unanswered. To lose you was unbearable, but no one can explain. Life and death hold mysteries but one thing's for sure, I loved you then and I love you now. Sleep tight, Kelsey ...'

I could see just by looking at Sean and Judy's faces, and the faces of their surviving brood, that life was never going to be the same again without their beautiful girl. It was difficult to find words as I faced those faces of all the people who loved this young woman who had been taken from them so young. I was thinking about the service all week beforehand. I knew the depth of the suffering and struggles the family had been through, and I felt it important to honour that without losing the Christian focus, the peace and love that the service should be portraying.

I felt I'd let them down as I hadn't found any of the answers they sought, so I needed to find some hope from somewhere. When I was in church on the morning of the funeral giving out food parcels, I found hope in the chancel light that burns on the High Altar underneath the three stained-glass windows. It burns 24 hours a day as a symbol that light always overcomes darkness.

That light still shines.

To us as Christians, it represents Jesus, nothing more complicated or simple than that. Jesus said, 'I am the light of the world,' and nothing will overcome Jesus, nothing at all. So, if anything can take the sting out of all that pain, suffering and torture the family have been put through, and are still going through, then it has to be the light of Jesus. But why Jesus? Well, he kept things simple. He gave us this really clear example to just love one another, to be kind, be patient and tolerant, and what I've seen of the family in the months that I've got to know the Devlins is that they are full of love, compassion and care.

It came to the part of the service where Kelsey's body would normally be commended to God's care. Of course, this funeral was as far from normal as it was possible to be. It was the first time I have ever led a service that was without the deceased's body, and I hope it will be the last.

The Christian perspective involves two key things: the commendation, which is the part where the body is commended to God, and the committal, which is the ashes to ashes, dust to dust bit, committing the body to God.

Being without Kelsey's body to say the sacred words over meant I had to change the liturgy and adapt the service. I felt it was important to fulfil the rites of a Christian funeral, the funeral liturgy and the committal to the ground, to the final resting place. We had no idea where Kelsey's resting place was, but I felt it was important to say the words, to uphold the ritual and to bring comfort to the family. It is a ritual that underpins the idea of resurrection, of eternal life through Jesus Christ.

The text tells us that death is a gate into a realm of eternal life, and that nothing can separate us from the love of God. Cleansed of sin, the deceased is commended to God and into blessed rest and eternal peace. What beautiful, sacred words.

By now, we were all crying. As the words in the service say: 'We shall not all die, but we shall be changed.' It even asks us to rejoice at the deceased being taken by God to be with him, turning 'the darkness of death into the dawn of new life'. Yet there had been no coffin at the church. There was no coffin to sprinkle holy water over, reminding us of the rite of baptism.

The words of Job 1:21 are so poignant and meaningful in light of the circumstances of Kelsey's death and the community she was part of. The verse says: 'Naked I came from my mother's womb, and naked I will depart. The Lord gave and the Lord has taken away; may the name of the Lord be praised.' In this, we are reminded that the only riches are spiritual riches as everything else falls away, and we leave this earth with nothing except for our souls. It is a beautiful reminder amid a place that struggles with itself, that is beloved of its people but is blighted by so much poverty and hardship.

Something about Kelsey's death and the tragic, unfathomable circumstances around it feels symbolic to me of the community I serve. There is a sense of people fighting against the odds, being the underdogs, of being ignored and underestimated. The Devlin family were being ignored by the authorities. No one in government appeared to be listening, because of who they were – or more accurately, who they weren't. But I loved them and I still do. To me, the family is the epitome of resilience despite their circumstances and their troubles. They are a wonderful representation of a loving family, and the love they all have for each other has been an honour to witness.

With every bone in my body, I wish I could give them the answers and the peace they crave, the answers I fear they will probably never receive. I don't know how and why Kelsey died. I don't know if it was a tragic illness or something darker. I can't say what happened, but I can say that it has been so cruel for the family, and incredibly sobering to me as an individual, to come up against immovable forces, the legal and government agencies that appear unable or unwilling to act on their behalf.

In a place of poverty, the loss of a person simply adds to the state of deprivation that people are already suffering. When you don't have enough food to put on the table, or when you exist in a state of depression or anxiety without spiritual wellbeing, then the gaps are filled by loved ones. When those nearest and dearest die, it leaves a huge hole in people's lives, especially when they have nothing else.

There is still so much taboo around talking about death and dying. Bereavement is something we struggle with talking about comfortably, and even more so in places of poverty where a lot of people are less equipped to deal with it, because they are already missing out on the richness and fullness of life. If you wake up in the morning dreading what lies ahead, and then a death is thrown into that scenario, it can place people in highly vulnerable, difficult and dark places. This is my fundamental understanding of the parish I serve, and places of deprivation in the wider sense. So much has already been taken away either by life circumstances, cycles of bad luck or poor health.

We consider death a private matter, but in the kind of urban setting that Burnley provides, then actually it becomes a public matter, and this can also be extremely hard for a grieving family, as well as being supportive. It can place a huge burden on that family to grieve in a certain way or to do things in a certain manner, making it even harder to cope with the situation. I have seen how the death of a family member or friend becomes a gap that widens for the people around them. Someone may have been the confidante, the lover or the family 'rock', and when they go they leave behind a tsunami of grief and loss that hits people hard. This is a discussion that needs to become part of a wider conversation about death and poverty. We need to start asking the question of where bereavement leaves people who have few choices and minimal support.

We should be looking at ways to fund support for the bereaved because I see here in Burnley, and I'm sure this is played out in the wider community, that people who struggle alone with loss turn to other ways of coping, such as through alcohol or drugs. People are trying to eradicate their feelings of grief, to numb the pain, and this seems commonplace when people have no other real support system. If there is no one who cares enough to help, or no one to lean on, then a bottle of wine or the smoke of a pipe must look attractive. I only have to look at my friend Mark to see the proof of that.

I believe this forms part of a wider conversation about drug use. Let's be honest, many people on our estates use soft drugs such as cannabis as a daily antidote to their circumstances. If you walk some of the streets of the parish, the scent of marijuana is as strong as the instinct for survival in the community. And where there is loss, there is also the cost of a funeral, which can run into thousands of pounds. Many people here are left to beg, borrow or steal to try to afford that.

Loan sharks may provide the only means to providing the kind of send-off that people aspire to, because, let me tell you, no one has that sort of money sitting around. If they can't find the money, then they're looking at a corporation funeral, which is a basic funeral service, and this can be the final hammer blow to many who would see this as deeply shameful.

People have pride. They may not have cash or possessions, but what they crave is dignity. Perhaps sometimes it is all they have, and so, for many, a council funeral would be unthinkable, which drives people to look into other ways to fund one, ways that potentially drive them into more poverty.

During the pandemic, our diocese removed all of our funeral fees so the Church of England in Lancashire didn't charge anything for a service. This was a wonderful gesture, but I do wonder if the funeral providers could have stepped up and helped out more during the horror of Covid 19. My personal fee for holding a service is £10, which basically just covers my petrol, so lifting that from a funeral that costs £3–4,000 is a fairly minimal gesture, though we actually received criticism from funeral directors in the area for waiving the fees. I understand they are businesses, but even so, when people are at their most vulnerable it's quite easy to say they want the best flowers, a horse and carriage, etc. I worry about how people in financially unstable situations like many of my parishioners find this kind of money. Quite possibly, it's from loan sharks, or other ways of borrowing, plunging people already in a fragile position deeper into debt. I know that round here, on the estates, there are ways to borrow off people who are not registered banks, though I don't know what kind of interest is charged. I suspect it's more than at NatWest.

When it came to Kelsey's funeral and my contact with the whole family, I felt like I was ministering at the very edges of my capability, as close to the edge as a human being can be, because it was crushing me, heart and soul.

I wasn't feeling the grief that the Devlin family were experiencing, but I was feeling the same anger and helplessness with the situation. I tried to create something they could cling on to, and all I could offer them was my faith that, whatever happened to Kelsey, she was now at peace and had gone to a better place.

I told the congregation that it was – it is – my belief that Kelsey's earthly journey may have ended but her spiritual journey hadn't. It is my belief that Kelsey's story will continue on somewhere else and will continue in a place where all the things that upset us, and cause so much pain and suffering, just won't exist, in a place where suffering simply doesn't happen.

After the ceremony, we all went outside. The wind was blowing and it had begun to drizzle, as if the sky itself were weeping, but we all stood and watched as a dove was released, symbolising eternal peace and hope. Balloons were also sent skywards and the family went on their way. I stayed behind in the church trying to process what had happened that day. Sometimes, I sit on a particular chair at the back of the church and that's what I did when they all left. When I was first sent to this church on placement, not having a clue I would go on to become the vicar here, I used to sit in a chair at the back gazing around the interior and trying to keep a low profile.

St Matthew's is a beautiful church. The stone columns that line each side of the aisle take the eye down to the High Altar, where a large gold cross sits on a purple silk altar cloth. Above the altar are the three stained-glass windows that depict Jesus as an infant, and above that is the star-shaped window, through which light pours into the space. Sometimes I sit here and contemplate, and sometimes I use it as a moment to pray, which is what I did that day. I prayed that God might send the Devlins some comfort and support. I knew the funeral service, such as it was, would be an important stepping stone on their way to some kind of acceptance, both of Kelsey's demise and of the nature of that death. Acceptance is a really important part of the grieving and recovery process.

'I just want my daughter to walk back through the door, with that cheeky grin of hers, and a McDonald's in her hand.

I just want to look at my phone and see a message from her, a heart emoji or somethin',' Judy had said during one of my many visits to her home.

'I just want the phone to ring, and to hear her voice at the other end of the call.'

As the grieving journey shifts and changes, there is an acceptance that the person won't ever come through the door, won't ever send a text or WhatsApp message, won't ever be at the end of the line asking what is for dinner. The Devlin family has to learn to live with the 'what ifs'. What if Kelsey hadn't travelled to Islamabad? What if someone had managed to see her in the hospital: would she still be alive? What if there was plenty of cash and they could bring her home?

Of course, none of the usual work and challenges in my ministry went away during this time. Mark reappeared and became a regular again at the Breakfast Club we were running each Saturday. The idea of the club is to provide a free egg or bacon butty and brew to anyone who wants one, at the same time as they collect their food parcel from the foodbank, which was now being held inside St Matthew's itself. He still looked an absolute mess, mind, but he was chatty and seemed okay.

'What's to do, Mark? Are ye alright?' I said, walking over to him with a proffered butty and a mug of milky coffee.

'I'll just have the coffee, thanks, Father. I can't really eat solid food no more,' Mark replied.

'Sorry to hear that. How's things with your GP?' I said, sitting down next to him as he sipped from the mug that shook slightly in his hand.

'Oh, they've given me the liquid drinks to have and they're keepin' me goin'.'

I was relieved to hear it.

'And have ye managed to cut down the alcohol?' I asked, guessing already what his reply might be.

'Well, it's hard, like. I'm tryin', Father Alex, I'm tryin' ...' Mark looked sheepish, but I was just glad to see him. I was grateful he had the church to come to for a chat and a brew, for no other reason than getting him away from the shithole he lived in for a few hours.

When he'd finished his brew, he turned to me.

'Father Alex?'

'Yes, Mark.'

'Have ye got three quid for a can?'

I sighed.

'No, Mark, I have not.'

15.

HOPE

'Even though I walk
through the darkest valley
I will fear no evil,
for you are with me ...'

Psalm 23, A Psalm of David

'Father Alex,' said the little girl Layla, who was tapping me on my shoulder.

I craned my neck round. I was sitting in a front-row seat with one of the classes from a primary school about to watch a performance of *Dick Whittington*. Excitement was at fever-pitch as this was the first time we'd been on a trip since Covid.

'Are ye alright?' I said, smiling.

The girl had blonde curls and big wide blue eyes.

'Father Alex, can I ask ye a question?' she lisped.

'Of course ye can, you can ask me anythin' you want,' I replied, still smiling.

'Is "dick" a swear word?' she whispered.

My heart almost stopped.

'Ooh, well, I'm not sure, but I think it's another word for "Richard". Will that do?' I replied, haltingly.

She looked at me, then nodded and sat back in her seat. I'd broken out in a sweat, but the performance started and I thought no more of it.

Halfway through, one of the characters said: '... for you are Richard, but I shall call you Dick!'

I felt a small hand on my shoulder this time, pulling at the fabric of the fluorescent jacket I wore as a volunteer.

'You were right, Father Alex! You were right!'

If there's hope to be found in the community I serve, it's where the young people are, and it's usually the simplest things that foster hope. The innocence of the kids as they watch a pantomime, the giggling and playing they do at Fun Church, the sheer life and energy of the kids I see each week in our schools.

Even my friend Jenny Swears-a-Lot was hopeful when she imparted some news to me which would've floored most people. I saw her at the anxiety group as usual, and this time she almost blew my socks off.

'What's to do, Jenny? Are ye alright?' I said when she walked in with her mates.

'Am I fuck!' she replied, spiritedly.

'What's goin' on?' I asked, sitting next to her in the circle of mostly women in the bright, cheerful room.

'Well, it's Harrison. They found a tumour when he broke his back, but they've operated and he's alright now,' she said, matter-of-factly, almost cheerfully I might have said.

'You're goin' to have to start again, Jenny, because I can't take all that in!' I exclaimed.

Jenny looked at me like I was being thick.

'He did a crab at school, ye know the thing they do when they lift themselves up in an arch from the floor like a crab? Well, he fell on his back. He only fell a foot or so, but when he came home he said his back was killin' him. For weeks he kept going on about this backache. He weren't screaming in pain, but I took him to doctor's anyway. Doctor said she thinks it's pulled muscles, and to come back in six weeks.'

'Sorry, is this your ten-year-old boy?' I said, trying to get a handle on this story.

'Yeah, Harrison. So, we did that and he was referred to a physiotherapist. We went to A&E five times, the physio two times. He was still playing football, badminton and kickboxing but he kept saying he was gettin' electric shocks down his legs. He played a football tournament but within three days he was walking like he'd had a stroke.

'We kept going back to A&E and the doctors, and eventually he was given an MRI at Blackburn Hospital, and the doctors told him not to move. He'd broken his back, and there was a tumour there as well on his spine. They blue-lighted him down to Manchester, then we were stuck in A&E for six hours with a child with a broken back.'

Jenny finished and took a swig from her can of fizzy pop.

I stared at her, incredulously.

'You're tellin' me that nobody thought to do an X-ray on your son's back or legs until that point?' I said eventually, stunned by this revelation.

'Yeah, that's right. It's like they weren't really listenin', but when they found it, it all happened very fast.'

'So, how's Harrison now?'

Jenny shrugged.

'He were in surgery for eleven hours. He was rait though, he was fine with everything. He said as long as he could play football he wasn't bothered.'

I've said it before, and I'll say it again. Lancastrian women are as strong as they come. What resilience. What bloody courage. I feel so much hope for Jenny's family, despite their problems, because they've got a mum who teaches them – and me – to take everything in their stride. It's the same for Judy. I see her at Fun Church every week and though I know she is grieving Kelsey deeply she is always bright, always helpful and nurturing to the youngsters. Her family has come to mean a great deal to me, and I have hope that they will get through their trauma and come out the other side stronger and wiser, and even more compassionate if that's possible.

I wish I could feel the same hope for my friend Mark. I really thought things might have turned a corner with him after the visit to the rehab facility, but that was until he dropped a bombshell about his new 'accommodation'. He came to Breakfast Club and started to tell me how skint he was because his place was costing him a fair chunk of his benefits.

'I'm sorry, tell me again, Mark. You're tellin' me you're paying £260 a month to live in a caravan with no running water or heating?'

I could feel my anger rising. Winter had set in and I worried about my friend constantly as the days and nights got colder.

'That's right, Father Alex. There's no toilet neither, so I 'ave to shit in a bucket,' Mark added.

I sat and stared at him.

'Alright, let's go and look at this accommodation. You're tellin' me the council is paying housing benefit to your

landlord for the privilege of you sleepin' in a disused caravan?' I queried, grabbing my coat.

'Pretty much.' Mark shrugged. Again, that shrug. It was
beginning to infuriate me.

'Let's go now. I want to see this palace you're payin' for,' I
said, jangling my keys and pointing to the door.

Mark got into my car. He smelt terrible, of stale beer and
stale body odour. It was very clear he had no washing facilities nor anywhere to clean his clothes. I couldn't believe this
was happening in twenty-first-century Britain.

The caravan was situated on the fringe of Burnley
town centre. Walking up to it, it barely looked fit for human
habitation. There was no lock on the door. There was no
gas, water or electricity. It was literally a dirty shell that
acted as shelter and little else. Mark was absolutely right, it
had no toilet. It was downright squalid, and I could've
screamed in frustration. How, in modern-day Britain, can a
landlord be allowed to receive payment without any purpose-
ful checks from a council that was indirectly paying for the
privilege?

'Right, that's it. We're goin' to the council,' I said, storming
off into my car. I waited for Mark to stumble over, then drove
us back into Burnley.

There was a long queue at the council office, but I was
determined to report Mark as homeless. I couldn't let him
return to that place, and I felt strongly something had to be
done. When our turn arrived, we were faced with an entirely
unenthusiastic advisor.

'I've come to report this man as homeless. He needs emer-
gency accommodation, and I won't be leavin' until he gets it,'
I said firmly.

The advisor, a lady in her forties, looked at us both and just pointed to a telephone less than a yard away from the counter.

'You need to ring that,' she said. 'Next!'

'Er, no, we haven't finished yet. What do you mean, I have to ring a phone that's been sitting here all along while we've been queuing?' I said.

I knew I sounded a bit stroppy and I didn't like being that way. This woman had probably seen a million sad stories and was probably ground down by them. Even so, it wasn't the help I hoped for.

'I'm sorry, but ye have to use that phone. Can ye move on, thanks,' she finished and was already staring past us at the person behind me.

I can't explain it, but I felt a surge of something like rage. Did no one care? Was there hope to be found in this environment? Was there hope that we'd be able to house Mark tonight rather than return him to his shit-box caravan?

After several attempts during which the phone rang and rang, someone eventually picked it up.

'Housing. Can I help?'

'Yes, I hope so. I've been told to call ye. I'm in the council offices with my friend Mark. He's a chronic alcoholic and he's been housed in the most appalling accommodation. He's basically homeless and he needs somewhere safe and clean to go ...'

As I spoke, I suddenly realised that everyone in the queue that still snaked down the offices could hear what I was saying. If this wasn't all humiliating enough for Mark, he had to put up with every Tom, Dick or Harry listening in.

'Listen, everyone here can hear us. Can we please speak privately?'

'Sorry, no, we can't do that,' said the voice at the other end of the phone. They just didn't give a stuff.

Later, after I'd registered Mark as homeless and returned him to that awful caravan, vowing to not rest until he was properly housed, I took to social media to call out what I considered to be shockingly uncaring treatment by council staff. Within half an hour of my posts landing on Twitter, someone who was able to make a difference got in touch. Magically, Mark's assessments were brought forward and a date set for him to enter sheltered accommodation, a move that could signal entry into inpatient detox.

Mark's situation prompted a conversation with a social worker, who got in touch with me as I was now his point of contact. She promised to investigate the caravan landlord and suggested that if life as a priest ever got too much, I should join Social Services. As high praise as that was, I said I was purely filling the gaps that Mark had fallen through, and I was disappointed that it fell to a priest to raise such concerns.

I know my friend is walking through the valley of darkness. It doesn't get much darker than addiction, and the catastrophic consequences it has had on Mark's well-being, and his life. I have vowed to walk beside him, to guide him if possible, but really to offer him whatever small hope I can that things might one day get better, may change for him.

Despite the continual challenges my parishioners like Mark face, I am usually a glass-half-full person and so I cannot help but feel hope both for my community and for my church and country.

But what does hope look like in these challenging times? I often wonder what it is that we should hope for collectively. Whether it should be a new age of peace and harmony, whether it should just be limited to an end to conflict and hunger. Whatever hope is, and whatever we hope for, there have been so many moments in my ministry that have made the darkness go away, even for a short time.

One of those moments was a telephone call I received from Sally and George, who had miscarried their baby so many months earlier.

'Father Alex?' I recognised the voice at the other end of the line but couldn't place it immediately.

'Yes, that's me. How can I help?' I replied, my brain whirring, one eye on the cat as she walked around my feet, wanting her breakfast.

'It's Sally. You came to see us and were so kind that we wanted ye to know we had a healthy baby girl two months ago, and we'd very much like her to be baptised at St Matthew's ...'

It took a minute to sink in, then I almost dropped the telephone receiver.

'You what?' I almost shouted, joy overtaking my ability to speak properly. 'That is the best news I've heard in a long time; congratulations both of you.'

'And that's not all,' she continued. 'We've decided to get married and we'd like to have our wedding at St Matthew's as well. Can we come and see ye to talk about it all?' Sally sounded so happy.

'Nothing would give me greater pleasure,' I said. 'Come and have a brew and we'll go from there,' I added, as we ended the call.

To say I was overjoyed was an understatement. To say it was a ray of light beaming into the darkness almost doesn't describe it. I cried with joy at the news.

These days, we can bring lots of hope into the work of St Matthew's church with the funding we received from generous donations made as a result of the BBC documentary. Almost £150,000 poured in over the months following the broadcast, which I am happy to say we have put to good use. We set up a committee with local stakeholders to best decide how that money could be spent, and as a result we have been able to support various individuals with counselling and mental health services. We have been able to explore a range of after-school clubs, including wellbeing groups and workshops. We have linked up with a mental health charity in Blackpool and can offer their services to our parishioners.

Yet there are always people whom we can't help, or who don't want to be helped.

A woman came into church recently. She'd started coming to Breakfast Club so I approached her and said hello, as I do. She was probably in her forties, and she looked alright. Her clothes and appearance were tidy enough and she had long brown hair pulled back into a pony tail.

'Are ye alright?' I said, going over.

'I'm alright, thanks,' she said, her hands trembling in that tell-tale way.

'Do ye need a hand?' I asked. 'It looks like you might need one.'

The woman smiled.

'I'm cluckin' a bit. Don't worry about me, I'm used to it. Been an addict for twenty-two years now. It's normal for me, like,' she said.

I'm always amazed when people come right out with it, and just say their piece. The term clucking refers to the physical symptoms of withdrawal, meaning she may not have her next supply of whatever she is taking.

'Well, I'm sorry to hear that. What's your name? I'm Father Alex.'

'I'm Suzanne, Father. It's alright, I've been like this a long time …'

I sat down next to her.

'Don't you ever think about gettin' clean?' I asked, hoping I wasn't being too intrusive as I'd only just met her.

'Not really, Father. I'm just grateful I don't have to run around to score any more.'

She made it sound like a real win.

'Suzanne, how easy is it to get drugs around here?' I was curious as this world that so many seemed to inhabit was largely invisible to me. She looked at me like I was mad, then burst into a throaty laugh.

'I could walk out of this door and within a hundred yards I could score five or six times,' she said, staring at me like I was an alien from another planet.

We both smiled, me in my naivety, her in her disbelief. Yet there was something about Suzanne. To be an addict for 22 years takes some resilience and strength. It takes a lot of energy and commitment to keep having to take drugs, to get money to buy them, to go and score, to risk being robbed, cheated or worse by a dealer, and then, finally, to take the substance, and after its effects have worn off to start the whole cycle again. I almost admired her. She looked chipper enough, and we parted company on a strangely uplifting note.

After a sleepless night worrying about Mark, I called Lancashire County Council to report him officially as a vulnerable adult. Perhaps I was overstepping the boundaries of a priest's responsibility, but if there is anything I have learnt over the years, it is that people are deeply valuable.

Here, in a deprived northern town, where the headlines usually scream poverty and destitution, there is also an undaunted spirit and an unwavering survival instinct. People here are stronger than you could ever imagine. I can name a dozen people off-hand who shouldn't be alive, yet they are. This isn't Eton, and so these people remain a source of untapped intelligence and humour. They are people who haven't had opportunities in life, and that alone is a travesty. There are kids here whom I know might be heading for prison one day, and there is nothing stopping them, there is no mechanism in place, nothing at all. At the same time, I know lots of wonderful parents doing their very best to raise good kids in extremely difficult circumstances.

What I don't do to my parishioners is throw out that old saying that Jesus loves them. I mean, he does, but they don't want to fucking hear that while their child is self-harming, and another has lost their job, and they're collecting tins of beans from our foodbank. They might be walking in that valley of darkness, but as Psalm 23:4 says, God is always there, Jesus is always present as a source of courage and hope.

I see little miracles all the time. At the moment, the cost-of-living crisis has affected donations to our foodbank. People who weren't on the edge are now facing decisions about heating their homes adequately or eating well, and we're finding they simply can't give in the way they used to. We've had days when our supplies are almost empty, and we've had to delve into our financial donations to buy food for people. Then, all of a sudden, a car will come around the corner or the phone will ring, and it's someone offering to drop off a load of food. That miracle has never failed in the whole time we've been running the scheme. Hope is a miracle in itself these days. Believing things will get better has become a radical stance to take.

16.

SALVATION

'Then said Jesus, "Father, forgive them, for they
do not know what they are doing."'

Luke 23:34

Where do I begin?

My salvation began the day I turned to the gospel of Jesus
and started to see that this was the way, the truth and the life
for me. It continued the day I took my first service as an
ordained deacon, dressing in the vestry amid the bustle of the
choir getting ready, pulling on the green chasuble vestment
with a stole worn diagonally across my chest to denote I was
still training and hadn't yet been priested.

I was nervous, but excited to be, at last, joining the thousands of clergy in the Anglian Communion worldwide who
have the privilege of becoming a form of connection between
their congregation and Jesus. Stepping out to face the congregation, my heart was thumping and my throat felt dry, but as
soon as I said the Lord's Prayer I felt redeemed, I felt liber-
ated.

I wonder if perhaps my salvation continues at Turf Moor, the place where I can truly feel like a disciple of the beautiful game and put away my dog collar for a few hours, immersed in the excitement and atmosphere of Burnley Football Club's stadium. As my daughter Holly and I walk to each home game, Holly sometimes wearing a club shirt, me with my hat and scarf (weather dependent, naturally) as well as a Claret and Blue jersey with 'Rev' printed on the back, and as we pass underneath the straight mile, the culvert above our heads carrying the Leeds–Liverpool Canal, we feel a kind of salvation, a redeeming of our humanity as part of the seething masses, drinking, shouting, laughing and swearing on their way to the match. We pass the Royal Dyche pub with everyone standing outside, pint in hand, and always say hello to local legend Rocky, a Claret fan who is at every game, come rain or shine.

'Alright, Rocky. Are ye alright?' I shout over.

'Can't fuckin' complain, Father!' the man in his late seventies shouts back.

Everyone knows Rocky. Rocky is hard to miss. He's the one giving a loud running commentary through the game, if you're lucky enough to stand near him.

Once we say hello to him, Holly and I invest in a Holland's meat pie, then we're ready to watch the match, and I become part of our community, rather than someone on the edge, trying to make a difference.

The salvation of the community I serve is a trickier one to predict. Every day there seems to be something happening to someone, some new drama unfolding, veering between comedy and absolute tragedy.

The woman whose daughter hanged herself came back to

the foodbank recently. I went straight over to her. In truth, I hadn't expected to see her again.

'How are ye? Are ye alright?' I said. 'Can I get you a brew or an egg butty?'

'Alright, Father Alex. Well, things haven't been easy,' she replied. She looked run down.

Her eyes still had dark shadows underneath them and she looked gaunt, as if she hadn't been looking after herself or eating much.

'I'm alright though. I've got new accommodation but it's a bit of a shit hole.' She laughed as if this was funny.

My heart sank.

'Sorry to hear that,' I said. 'What's to do?'

'Yeah, so it was infested with ants. The bloody things were everywhere. The landlord said I had to sort it out meself, so I did, like, but I had to pay for it.'

She told me where the flat was that she was renting, and it was a road I knew well on the other side of Burnley, somewhere sex workers and clients often frequented, and with a reputation for drug using and dealing.

This lady, who has been through so much, can never, even for a moment, leave behind her circumstances. I knew without her having to tell me that this flat, which already had an ant infestation, would most likely be pretty threadbare and probably had not been well maintained. She probably had only the very basics in furniture and food, because she was forced to use our foodbank, and when she stepped outside her front door, she was greeted by the further realities of her life: crime, drugs and anti-social behaviour all around her.

I honestly don't know how she, or any of the people I regularly deal with, survive. Sometimes, I don't even know why they'd want to. People are living in dangerously abnormal ways, and the impact on the wider community must be cata-strophic.

There's a guy whose name I don't know, who sometimes comes in on a Saturday, sits at the back of the church, and cries. I have tried to approach him, but he never wants to speak, and I respect that completely, so we just leave him be, to do what he needs to do. I never see him at the services nor during the week, just on Saturdays. He is middle-aged, a pleasant-looking man who is well presented and quiet. He reminds me of an Evel Knievel toy I had as a child. I would wind him up and up and up until he went ping. I don't know whether it's a good thing that he comes here to let it all out or whether it shows a real sadness in his life that just cannot be expressed openly. Either way, the doors of my church will always be open to him, whether he wants to talk or not, or pray or not.

But what does salvation mean? And perhaps more impor-tantly, how do we go about getting some? A quick look online, and one of the definitions offered is the state of being saved or protected from harm or a dire situation. By now, I think you can see that many of my parishioners live in a place of needing some kind of spiritual protection. They need compassion, safety, trust and love to be shown to them. They need their worries and fears to be heard and understood.

To my mind, salvation is something offered spiritually during Holy Communion. Holy Communion is the ceremony in which the community comes together and experiences direct communion with God with the bread and wine. It always strikes me as a time of sharing something special, whether you believe in transubstantiation – the wine literally turning to the blood of Christ, the bread to his flesh – or not. I don't believe that this literally occurs. I am a liberal Christian, and I see it as a beautiful metaphor that Christ is within us, and we can be touched by him during this sacred ceremony, yet it has become hugely significant in the tradition I am part of.

We have Prayers of Intercession during Holy Communion, where we pray for the whole community and the whole of the Church in the world. We pray for the sick, which can take a while as we have an ageing congregation. We also pray for the dead and the bereaved. In a mad, crazy world, I find that Holy Communion is the perfect antidote to rampant consumerism and the self-centred nature of contemporary culture with its selfies, perfect Instagram images and have-it-now access to pretty much anything if you have the money.

As a Christian, it is really important to me to have God in my life, to be anointed by something, and to feel I am actively joining the house of God. Before that, I will offer the prayer of absolution, via which, through the priest, God forgives people for their sins. It is a privilege to be that conduit, though it is the peace of God that is offered, not forgiveness from me. Holy Communion is a time of relationship, a time of being in the presence of God, a time of saying sorry, and of actively asking for forgiveness. It is as close to salvation as I am able to offer as a conduit of Jesus' love, and it is a special service that has always meant a lot to me.

At Argos, I had a Time Planning Grid, with four boxes to sort out which tasks needed doing. The first box was the 'Nice to Do' box, the second was the 'Must Do' box, the third was the 'Must Do Now' box and the last was simply called 'Oh Shit'.

Sometimes I wonder if the future of the Church of England will, very soon, sit in that last box, unless we find a way to become more outward-looking, to discuss differences better among ourselves and to open ourselves up to the talents and skills of people who don't fit the prescribed model of what a Christian might be. Christians aren't white-middle-class people from Hertfordshire; they're more likely these days to be a kid on an estate in Moss Side, or the black family worshipping in Tottenham, London.

Most of the people I come into contact with on a daily basis would probably be placed in the 'Oh Shit' box, too. They're not easy or 'nice' to deal with, with their complex needs and problems.

Mark is permanently in the 'Oh Shit' box. He's been playing silly beggars with me recently, and I have been in touch with the local council more times than I can recall over the past weeks and months.

'Alex, it's the bishop ...' Sarah poked her head around my office door recently.

'Oh shit,' I replied, fervently hoping my wife had her hand over the receiver.

'Hello Bishop Philip, how are ye? Are ye alright?' I said, knowing I was going to get a bollocking.

'Father Alex, why am I getting complaints from the council about you kicking off at them?' said the Bishop of Burnley, Philip North, a man I hold in the highest esteem.

'Er, well, that's probably because I have been kicking off quite a lot,' I said, cringing.

'Why don't you tell me why ...?'

'Do ye remember the guy Mark who I reported to the council and Social Services as a vulnerable adult more than a month ago?' I started. I was greeted with silence so I carried on.

'Well, nothin' has been done, or should I say nothin' useful for Mark. The council came and took away the sofa he was sleeping on so he's now sleeping rough on the ground. When I found out, I went down there in my car to find him and, sure enough, he was still homeless and in the worst state I'd ever seen him. He hadn't been to the supported accommodation and nobody thought to look for him, so I kicked off, Bishop. I emailed every county councillor in Burnley and I told them they have a duty to care for him ...'

My voice trailed off.

'I see,' said the bishop.

Heartened by even this small interaction, I went on.

'Finally, and because I had to kick off, they've joined the dots so that Housing is speaking to Social Services and they've found him accommodation, though it's above a pub ... at least it's something, and they're goin' round to see him now and checking he's alright.'

Sarah looked at me from the lounge door.

'Well then, carry on kicking off, Father Alex. You need to be a voice for the voiceless.'

The relief was intense, though I knew myself well enough to understand that even if the bishop had told me to stop helping Mark I wasn't sure I could. These people have got under my skin, in all their wonderful, sometimes eccentric, sometimes offensive glory.

I have experienced this community farting loudly through church services. I have people coming up to me and loudly informing me about the state of their cystitis or haemorrhoids. I have people coming for baptisms who have given their children bizarre names, such as the young couple whom I went to see in their council flat on the Stoops estate not long after I started my ministry.

'Can ye spell that?' I asked them, both with tattoos, both in their early twenties.

'S H E L L I S E,' the woman said nonchalantly.

'That's an unusual name,' I said, trying to make conversation.

'Yeah, well is was meant to be Chelsea, after his team, but the tattooist spelt it wrong …'

The man, probably only in his early twenties, pushed up his sleeve to reveal a tattoo, which did indeed spell Shellise.

'Rather than change it, we decided to change her name instead.'

If that wasn't bizarre enough, I was getting names of the godparents for another young couple's baby one summer day not long after.

'Vicky, oh, is that short for Victoria?' I asked, scribbling down the names. I was sitting on a large leather sofa inside a tiny lounge.

Between the sofa and the telly there was very little space and we were all squashed up together.

'Yeah, but you can't call her Victoria,' the woman called Lisa replied.

'Why not?' I said, not really thinking about it.

'Because she's a lesbian.'

I started to laugh.

'How does that work?' I looked up at her from my notepad.

'She doesn't like it,' she said matter-of-factly. 'If you call her "Victoria" she'll probably kick your head in.'

'She obviously feels very strongly about it. I'll make a note,' I replied, wondering where on earth I'd washed up.

There are so many awkward moments, so many tricky decisions to make as a priest. Sometimes the situations I've found myself in over the years dumbfound me. One of the most bizarre was going to see a lady who'd lost her husband. She was elderly herself, and so I went around, dog collar on, not sure what to expect.

'I'm Father Alex, I'm sorry for your loss,' I said as a woman opened the door. She was younger than I expected.

'Oh, it's not me, Father; she's upstairs. Just go t'top of the house. I'm just helpin' out.'

I walked into the corridor and glanced at a glass cabinet sitting in the lounge, which was pride of place. Inside it was a figurine of Elvis standing next to a statue of the blessed Virgin Mary. What wonderful reverence for both Mary and Elvis, I thought, seeing them, standing together on the same shelf, in the same cabinet.

I started climbing the narrow stairs in the terraced house and as I went up I was suddenly assaulted by a terrible smell. Oh dear, that's grim, I thought to myself, but I kept going, and as I did so it got stronger and stronger. By the time I got into the lady's room it was overwhelming. At the door, she called to me from her bed.

'Oh Father, I'm so glad you're here. Come and sit down.'

I walked in and the only chair in the room was her commode. I didn't make the connection until I reached the commode and saw a deposit in there. I couldn't bring myself to put the lid down and sit there, so I sat on her bed, as she thanked me for coming, quite oblivious to the odour.

At times like this, I concentrate on doing the right thing by someone. It took all my willpower to stay there and offer prayers for her departed husband and begin the funeral arrangements.

The Church and church life gives us all so much. Many of the things we celebrate in society, the festivals we enjoy, are deeply rooted in the Christian faith: Easter, Pancake Day or Shrove Tuesday, Harvest and Advent or Christmas. Lent and Easter have deeply significant meanings, and we sing about ploughing the fields and scattering seeds to grow food, which we still gather as a community to share among us. The things we celebrate wouldn't be there without our church, yet at the same time it is this church that is in danger of becoming irrelevant.

Where does all this leave our state church? What even is the role of Christianity in contemporary society? I believe the time has come to ask hard questions of our church and of our faith. Jesus said everything is possible for one who believes, and I believe in the Church of England, though it is a relationship that perhaps needs some intense counselling. Being part of the Church is a kind of love affair. There are times I feel exhausted by this relationship, though nowhere near as exhausted as the people who come to me for help, I'm sure.

My relationship with the Church of England is a bit like telling my wife one minute that I love her dearly, and the next, slapping her round the face with a wet fish. Let's just say, it's complicated.

At Argos, I used the 'shit sandwich' delivery method to give people bad news. I would tell them something good, then something catastrophic, then finish with something good again. I sometimes wonder if that's how it is with the Church as well.

Looking at the Church of England website, I can see all the brilliant things the Church does. It has 4,664 schools, and there are probably 15 million people alive today who have been through a Church of England education. That's a remarkable thing, and it gives me a real sense of optimism. And yet, the shit part is that most faith-related stories in the press seem to hover somewhere at the extremes, be it theological disagreements about same-sex relationships, declining church numbers or highly damaging horror stories of child abuse and bullying inside the Church. The reality for many people of faith is that they are good people doing their best in service and prayer to truly live out the values of Jesus Christ.

The Church was in the public arena again recently with the Archbishop of Canterbury speaking out about government plans to send refugees to Rwanda. He has been both celebrated and castigated for it.

The Most Reverend Justin Welby criticised the move, which has also been condemned by human rights groups and the United Nations, saying the plan is 'opposite the nature of God'. He said: 'It cannot carry the weight of our national responsibility as a country formed by Christian values, because subcontracting our responsibilities, even to a country that seeks to do well like Rwanda, is the opposite of the nature of God who himself took responsibility for our failures.'

I was really pleased that the Church was in the news about something of such huge importance, especially something that's not about the inadequacies and shortcomings of the Church of England, because that's where the Church should be. Neither the Church nor Christian ministers are there to placate politicians. They are there to challenge injustice. I'm very comfortable giving my two-penn'orth about the performance of our prime minister, just as I am about the performance of the Opposition. It's really important that the Church and Christian ministers are political but it's equally important to be non-partisan.

Our role is to call out injustice and it doesn't matter who is perpetuating that, so I applaud Justin Welby for taking a stand. What he did was to raise discussion concerning the wellbeing of those affected by these plans, meaning the Church is actually saying something that has direct relevance to a part of our society. Justin Welby is not the Church, though. For Christians who are prepared to put their head above the parapet there will always be criticism and ridicule. But why should this be?

It's because ministers are human beings, and we're as broken and as disorganised as the next person. You could put 20 Christians in a room and you'd get 20 different explanations of what it is to be a good Christian. Some would say you have to follow the Bible. Some would say you have to have a heart for the gospel. Some would say you have to role-model Jesus. I have no doubt in my mind, if there is to be criticism of this book, it will be from the Christian community, who will pick me up for the use of the text, or taking verses out of context, or failing to say this or that about the gospel.

I've felt for a long time there is a lack of confidence within the Church. I felt that even from the first times I went to Reverend Richard's services. Congregation numbers have been declining, which has created a sense of apathy and a reluctance to try new stuff, to have a go or attempt to change things.

When I was first ordained, Bishop Philip told me to try things and to risk failure. He actually said that what the Church needs is a 'bloody good cock-up' because actually at least then we'd be doing something. I think many people in the Church feel that the Christian ethos to be more loving translates into not challenging things, but I think that's wrong. It's vital to challenge policies that may cause injustice.

If we truly believe Jesus' words then we absolutely have to stand up and speak out with integrity, humility and honesty. If you truly believe what Jesus preached, it involves speaking out, just as he did. You don't have to be religious to have these values. My mum and dad taught me to speak the truth, to be honest and reliable, and to have integrity. When I walk the dogs, I listen to LBC Radio as I'm a big fan of presenter Shelagh Fogarty. I remember, day after day, listening to conversations about Brexit, thinking, *Will this never change?* Then we were hit by the pandemic and *everything* changed. The stories I've told, expressing some of the struggles people have had during the pandemic, and those I've observed and witnessed, reveal the anxiety, uncertainty and fear in many people about what the future holds. I've felt those things as well. I sit in my armchair at night and think, *Oh my goodness me, will this ever end?*

I recently held an assembly at one of our schools about my favourite story in the Bible, which is the one of Saul's conversion to Paul. The story of Saul's conversion is a reminder to us all that even when we're strongly opposed to something, whether that's Brexit, fishing quotas in the English Channel or whatever, we have all got the capacity to listen, and we have all got the capacity to change.

The Church needs to be seen as more loving and less divisive, more caring and less exclusive. It needs itself to have some kind of salvation, some kind of forgiveness both within the structure of the Church and in the greater community. The Church of England needs to be more inclusive and welcoming, and this all comes back to my views on same-sex relationships and sexuality. People who would argue the Bible tells us what to do are effectively saying we can't change because the Bible says x, y or z. But Saul changed and became a wonderful disciple of Jesus, and we need more disciples, we need more people to change.

I feel our country is crying out for Christianity, and more than this, that we're in danger of losing our identity as a Christian nation. Where I understand there is growth in Christianity in the UK is in London because of the diversity of cultures.

We can't rely upon churches filled with Hyacinth Bucket characters to take the Church into the 2050s and beyond. Christianity needs to be diverse. It needs to connect with Christians of different colour, background, creed and sexuality who are residing in this country.

The secular education system has an important part to play in this reconnection with our national faith, which I feel is so timely and important. We are a nation that is rethinking itself. We've been battered and bruised through so much trauma in recent years, and we are at a crossroads, if you like. We could become more marginalised, more 'look after ourselves' about things, or we could open our hearts and minds and create real change in society. Part of this could be achieved by providing a decent religious education for our children. The state education syllabus is pretty poor as things stand.

If this is truly a country of freedom of speech and thoughts, then we should at least give the opportunity to our young people to hear the stories, to understand and learn about Jesus and his teachings. I've just watched *The Pilgrimage*, as various celebrities follow in the footsteps of Saint Columbus. Our kids will never hear about these stories if they're not taught them: stories like Jonah and the Whale, Noah and his Ark, and Adam and Eve, to name just a few. I don't mean we should indoctrinate our kids, but we should share our knowledge with them so they can learn more if they wish. Schools seem to teach baby Jesus in the crib at Christmas and Jesus on the cross at Easter, and that's the syllabus fulfilled in many secular schools.

I believe the media also has a big role to play. Through Holy Week, you wouldn't have known it was happening in the UK if you turned on the telly or radio. Compare that to the coverage in other Christian countries, and you'll see that faith just isn't embedded within contemporary culture here. I think it should be.

Going back to my time in retail, Slade's 'Merry Christmas Everybody' was played on the sound system in September in my shop, showing that the commercial aspect of Advent has pushed Christianity to the fringes. There are reasons for this. The abuse revelations we've seen over the years are one of the reasons the Church exists on the sidelines in many places. It has been seen to be an institution of abuse, misogyny and corruption, and nobody has had the strength to say that these terrible things happen in lots of institutions as well as the Church. It has happened in the NHS, and in Government.

I don't think the Church has been open and honest about these things. Isn't it time to get all the skeletons out of the closet? If there are any still in there, get them out, make it known and apologise! This way, forgiveness and healing can happen.

It's important to say that while we acknowledge the past, it's also true that we're not personally responsible for what happened. I can apologise for what has been done to people in the past and at the same time understand that I'm not to blame. You can't go back and change what happened yesterday, but you can go ahead and influence what happens next. The Church has got to crack on. It has got to speak up, speak out, be proud, be confident, and argue better among ourselves before it's too late, because I don't think it's far off being too late.

There are many Anglican churches that are now in a state of palliative care and that really saddens me. We've got a lot to be positive about; we do a lot of brilliant things. Millions of children are educated by the Church of England. Millions of Christians and people of faith, Muslims and Jews, do so much for communities, with foodbanks and educational visits, etc. I think we do that stuff really well, but we need to reach out and offer spiritual wellbeing also, as perhaps that part of our message gets lost.

So many people today are spiritually unwell. I see that in the parish all the time. My aim is to help people get to a place where they might think about spiritual things. I've had so many conversations in my ministry about wellbeing. Father Alex, will everything be alright? Father Alex, is my mum in heaven? Father Alex, where's God in Brexit? In Ukraine? I'm not saying the answers I give are the right answers, but I hope they're from a place of humble honesty and integrity. I tell them what I believe. My job is not to indoctrinate people with the gospel, it's to invite them to come and see what's on offer from a loving God. There's a wonderful verse we encountered earlier at the start of Chapter 6: 'Come to me, all you who are weary and burdened, and I will give you rest.' The invitation is there.

All faiths have an important part to play in society, and we'd be so much poorer on so many levels if faith wasn't there.

My faith gives me hope. It gives me optimism. It gives me structure and a role model so that, when I am let down by politicians on a weekly basis, I have an example in Jesus who doesn't ever let me down, and who gives me words to live by, though not many, admittedly. Jesus doesn't say an awful lot in the Bible, but what he says is worth listening to, and it's a great framework to somebody that's going through a life of joy or a life of trauma.

My life has been traumatic, the stories I've been privileged to share here show that. There are times when I've thought the stories shared with me are going to break me, never mind the people going through this stuff. And in some ways, they have brought me to my knees, but never in a way that would make me reject my faith.

I'm not an aspirational priest. I feel immense joy and pride in serving my community, hearing the different stories, meeting different people, understanding different lives, and I only ever come to the same conclusion: that all human life is precious.

In terms of my own life, I have been through personal tragedy – the loss of a baby, and the death of my father from

dementia that left him unable to recognise his own family –
and yet I know God never abandons me. My real work,
however, is always going to be in sharing the gospel, and
helping those in need. I want to play my part in how the
future plays out for our national church. I want to be one of
the voices who speaks on behalf of the voiceless, just as my
bishop has urged me to do, who challenges prevailing political ideology and morality. Jesus begged for his father to
forgive the Roman soldiers who were crucifying him on the
cross. The saying, 'Father, forgive them; for they know not
what they do,' is known as the Word of Forgiveness. We all
need forgiveness. Not one of us is pure in heart and spirit, yet
Jesus tells us that, whatever we do, we are worthy of forgiveness, of salvation.

As I finish this book, the lives of my parishioners ebb and
flow. My foodbank has become something beyond just giving
out food to people who need it. It's a pop-up medical centre
at times, a counselling suite, a sanctuary for some, and I
cannot help asking the question, 'Why is this? Why are these
services falling to the Church, to a vicar?'

I see Jenny at the group frequently, and she's getting on
with her life, looking after her kids the best way she knows
how. Judy is still grieving, but she is holding her family
together, containing the grief of all her surviving nine children
and her new grandchildren. Somehow, she keeps going.

Mark went missing for a few days and so I rang the council
again and told them they should've jumped in their car and
gone to look for him, which is what I did. He was found,
thank goodness, but is in a bad way, and he is never not in
my prayers. There is light at the end of the tunnel as he has
been housed in a place called Gateway in Burnley, a charity

that offers support to homeless people, and has been accepted for inpatient detox, though we don't yet know when that will be.

Julie is an incredible and valued member of our congregation now, a shining light, and the baptism of Sally and George's baby went ahead and was a delight. We mentioned their loss, and how things can feel very bleak, but somehow, the sun comes out again from behind the clouds.

As for everyone else, they're in and out. Sometimes I see people, but many move on, including Gary and Suzanne and so many like them, continuing elsewhere the cycles of poverty and homelessness, of deprivation and addiction, sofa surfing and eking out some kind of living, and my prayers are with them too.

Rosemary, Ian and their large brood still come to church and I hope and pray they will find a way to change things together, to get the twins into some kind of education in the future.

Kelsey's dad Sean comes by the church and we talk and pray together. To date, no one from any agency or department has ever rung the Devlin family. Sean tells me I'm the only one who cared, and I have to tell him that it isn't me per se, I just represent the Church, our Church, the Church that exists for everyone.

EPILOGUE

STARFISH

'The moral of the story is,
never go for coffee with a vicar.'

Reverend Richard

I hope this book is a love letter, both to the North and to the people of our urban estates, very much including my beloved Burnley, and to the Church of England itself. Both have their problems, yet I love them with passion, and continue to serve them with everything I have as a person, and as a priest. Essentially, this book isn't about either, though. The main star of the show has always been Jesus Christ himself, and the teachings he gave us in the hope we could make a better world. It saddens me to think we need those teachings just as much today as perhaps we did 2,000 years ago when his feet walked upon this earth.

At the time of writing, it has just been Easter, which for Christians is an extremely special time at which we mourn the death of Christ and we celebrate his rebirth, and the whole idea of transformation and renewal.

My Holy Week services were quiet this year, and I wondered if God had been holding back to give me some kind of revelation, because on Easter morning we were full. Looking around the congregation, I realised that everyone was there. Everyone who has been a member of St Matthew's for forty-plus years. Everyone who comes to Fun Church, including loads of kids, were there. Most people from this book were there as well, including Mark, who arrived 10 minutes late as he always does. He crept in at the back of the church, but I saw him arrive. He instantly alienated himself from the rest of the congregation by sitting at a table, not in the chairs like everyone else.

When it came to intercessions, and by that I mean the Intercessory Prayer where we ask God for healing or help on behalf of others, I didn't mention my friend by name, but I was praying for him as well as many others. After the service, he came up to me in tears as if he knew what I'd done.

'Ye fuckin' made me cry,' he said.

Who else would say that on one of the holiest days of the year, if not Mark?

God had brought together the whole community, including all those brave enough to share their stories and hardships within these pages. It felt like a sign that we were meant to be writing this book, that we are meant to be having this conversation about the poor, about society, about contemporary Britain and who we think we are.

It feels like we are meant to be courageous, to say that Christianity and its message of love and peace to all should be part of our national conversations and wider discussions as we untangle the tragedies of the past few years and work out how the hell we're going to get through the immediate future.

We are a nation on the brink, or so it feels. On the brink of what, I cannot tell, but I fervently hope it's something like a new beginning, with inclusivity and fairness, compassion and spirituality leading the way through the troubled waters and storm clouds ahead.

That Easter service was incredibly special. The day had dawned sunny, the beautiful cherry blossom tree outside the church had burst into full bloom, and afterwards we all sat together and had a brew and a biscuit, and for the first time in a long time I felt uplifted. It's been a slog to get here. The past few years have been difficult for everyone, priests included. We're human beings and we have our own families and troubles, though I count my position to be one of huge privilege, affording me as it does the human connection and trust of my congregation and parishioners. But we're not immune from feeling emotions such as sadness and anger, as I've probably demonstrated throughout this book. All that, though, falls away when I'm surrounded by the community we have built here in Burnley, just as it is, without any need to change or modify any of it in any way.

If I'd have written a vision statement for my church, like I used to have to do at Argos, then it would have looked something like that service: everyone together in sacred community.

I don't want to paint Burnley as a place just of poverty and neglect – it is also a place of outstanding natural beauty – but I am confronted by these social ills every time I step foot outside the vicarage. Men stand around on street corners with cans of beer. There are fights and at night you see lads on bikes with backpacks and no lights, up to no good. We know that addicts come to the foodbank or breakfast just to get hold of jars of coffee, which they can sell for enough to buy crack.

Yet I believe in miracles and in the power of transformation. With the right support, urban communities can grow and change – and leave behind many of the problems they face. It is our job as people of faith, whichever religion we follow, to foster hope in our congregations, to gain people's trust and to instil optimism where there has been none. It isn't our job to lie to people and say that everything will be okay. We have to be honest. We cannot promise to fix people or situations, but we can shine a light of faith and hope in the darkness.

Mark keeps asking me to this day: 'Can ye make me better?' And I have to reply that I can't, it has to come from him, but I will support him every step of the way, and I pray for him every day.

Jenny carries on, looking after her kids, laughing in that throaty too-many-cigarettes way that she does, seemingly unphased by her troubles.

Judy Devlin is the same. She stopped me in the butcher's queue the other day and whispered she could get me five pies for £2 instead of what I was paying for our meat delicacies. I told her she was alright, but I appreciated the gesture.

People look out for each other up here, and I hope that never changes.

Perhaps we need to return to good, old-fashioned family values passed down through the generations where we care for our neighbours and friends, just like that first sermon I heard that put me on the path to my priesthood. Yet we have so much trauma on our estates, so much violence, chaos, gambling, addictions and poverty, that it can seem like an insurmountable task to make any headway.

I'm not a trained social worker, I'm just an ex-shopkeeper, a lousy stand-up comedian, a failed footie referee, and, finally, a vicar who loves his parish. I don't feel as though I'm overly equipped to deal with many of the things that my parishioners have to face, so I bring what I can: compassion, listening, care, the gospel of Jesus Christ and my faith.

Yet I didn't go into the priesthood to be a sales rep for the Church. If God wants people to come to St Matthew's then they'll come, and my part in that is to build good and strong relationships, which in turn create a platform for success. I still battle with my own demons, with the imposter syndrome that rears up, the voice in my head that tells me I'm thick or I'm the wrong person for the job. I am well aware of my limitations. I can't transform people's lives on a grand scale – and sometimes the sadness and suffering I see threatens to overwhelm me too.

As people of faith, whether we are Christian, Muslim, Jewish or any other religion, we have an opportunity in our communities to make a difference, even if we cannot hope to save all those who need our help. We have a chance right now to live in a new way, to place our faith at the heart of everything we do. I would go further and say it is time we all did this, believer or not, because there are struggles ahead. Conflict, climate change, cost-of-living price hikes, poverty, corruption, greed. I could go on.

Reverend Richard, the man who shepherded me into the priesthood all those years ago, gave me so much wonderful advice, but as I come to the end of this book I return to the sage wisdom of my old Argos Regional Manager, a guy called Steve Farndale, who once told me, and a room full of store managers, a story about some stranded starfish. It went something like this.

A father and his young daughter were out walking when they came to a beach upon which were thousands of starfish stranded upon the sand. The dad started to pick them up one by one and throw them back into the ocean.

The young girl said: 'What are you doing?' and the father replied: 'I'm throwing them back in, can't you see?'

The girl nodded but added: 'There are thousands. How can you possibly make a difference?'

As the man kept picking one up and throwing it back into the waves, he said: 'Well, I made a difference to that one, and that one, and that one …'

The pastures in the estates, across the urban terraces and streets, are most definitely not green, and their waters are often turbulent, but my soul is refreshed in having the privilege of serving them. God guided me, in the form of that friendly vicar who became a good friend, into the priesthood, though it was not an easy journey.

Going back to that man with the washing machine on his bike, there is everything you need to know about Burnley people. There is pathos, determination, comedy and tragedy all wrapped up in that incident. If I hadn't fallen in love already with the parish, that was the moment I did. Burnley is a place of tragedy – and comedy. It is an area forgotten by the wider world. It is blighted by high unemployment, poverty, addiction and council estates dotted with rusting old cars and rubbish. It is also a place of fierce community, of that bleak northern sense of humour that only living here will give you, and real humility. These people are part of me, as I am one of them, and as their vicar I'm entrusted with the 17,000 souls that live in the vicinity of St Matthew the Apostle Church.

It is an honour to serve them.

ACKNOWLEDGEMENTS

A few people have been pivotal in my life and career and have made the book possible. First, as regards the book itself, I extend my gratitude to Cathryn Kemp for her craft and my agent Jane Graham Maw for making it all happen. Alastair Campbell generously donated the foreword, and all my guests on The God Cast have provided stimulating conversation which has informed my thinking. I would also like to thank HarperNorth for being a joy to work with.

The real heroes of this book are the volunteers at food-banks and food pantries, supporters of homeless charities everywhere, and those who work to alleviate the problems of people living with addiction. They deserve every bit of praise.

From Argos: Paul Fitton (for his trust), Vicky Armstrong, Steve Farndale, Paul Long, Sandra Bennett, Lizzy Baker, Mark Broome, Whitto, DK, Kell, Macca, JD, Netty and Cheree. For those I had the privilege to lead in, Accrington, Blackburn, Rochdale, Manchester, Huddersfield and Burnley, thanks for the massive laughs and the long-lasting memories.

From Church: Bishop Philip North, Rev Richard Adams, Rev Kat Gregory-Witham, Rev Rie Walker, Fr Mark Williams,

Fr David Stephenson, Mr Enid Briggs and Rev Tracy Swindells. Also, Pastor Mick Fleming from Church on the Street Ministries and especially the Parish of St Matthew's, Burnley, where I serve as Vicar.

From the BBC: Ed Thomas, Phil Eddo, Louise Martin.

From Depeche Mode: Dave Gahan, Martin Gore, Alan Wilder, and Andrew Fletcher (RIP).

Huge thanks to my dearest mate, Rev Chris Krawiec and my oldest mates, Glynn Skelton and Kathryn Wrennall.

To the memory of my father, John, and my grandmother, Irene, who made me what I am and who I miss very much.

To my children, Joe, Holly and Rachel, and to my amazing, beautiful wife Sarah: thank you for being part of the journey, without you I am nothing. I love you. To my brother Robert – and his family Denise, Milly and Charlotte Frost – for his loyalty and their encouragement. And especially to my dearest mother, Pauline, for her unconditional love always. To Sheila and Alan and my extended family, Cathy and Graham, Jonathan and the entire Blackburn family.

And finally, to God, for calling me to this ministry, and for opening the door to an amazing adventure.

Thanks, and much love to all of you.

Harper
North

BOOK CREDITS

HarperNorth would like to thank the following staff
and contributors for their involvement in making
this book a reality:

Laura Amos
Hannah Avery
Fionnuala Barrett
Caroline Bovey
Charlotte Brown
Sarah Burke
Alan Cracknell
Jonathan de Peyer
Aya Daghem
Andrew Davis
Anna Derkacz
Tom Dunstan
Kate Elton
Mick Fawcett
Nick Fawcett
Simon Gerratt
Monica Green
Lauren Harris

Tara Hiatt
Ben Hurd
Megan Jones
Jean-Marie Kelly
Oliver Malcolm
Alice Murphy-Pyle
Adam Murray
Genevieve Pegg
Agnes Rigou
James Ryan
Florence Shepherd
Zoe Shine
Eleanor Slater
Emma Sullivan
Katrina Troy
Phillipa Walker
Daisy Watt
Kelly Webster

For more unmissable reads,
sign up to the HarperNorth newsletter at
www.harpernorth.co.uk

or find us on Twitter at
@HarperNorthUK

Harper
North